Modern Critical Interpretations

Fanny Burney's
Evelina

Modern Critical Interpretations

These and other titles in preparation

Fanny Burney's
Evelina

Edited and with an introduction by
Harold Bloom
Sterling Professor of the Humanities
Yale University

Chelsea House Publishers ◊ *1988*
NEW YORK ◊ NEW HAVEN ◊ PHILADELPHIA

© 1988 by Chelsea House Publishers,
a division of Chelsea House Educational Communications, Inc.,
  95 Madison Avenue, New York, NY 10016
  345 Whitney Avenue, New Haven, CT 06511
  5068B West Chester Pike, Edgemont, PA 19028

Introduction © 1988 by Harold Bloom

Printed and bound in the United States of America

10 9 8 7 6 5 4 3 2 1

∞ The paper used in this publication meets the minimum
requirements of the American National Standard for Permanence
of Paper for Printed Library Materials, Z39.48–1984.

Library of Congress Cataloging-in-Publication Data
Fanny Burney's Evelina.
    (Modern critical interpretations)
    Bibliography: p.
    Includes index.
    1. Burney, Fanny, 1752–1840. Evelina.   I. Bloom,
Harold.   II. Series.
PR3316.A4E834   1988   823'.6   87–23932
ISBN 0–87754–448–4 (alk. paper)

Contents

Editor's Note

This book brings together a representative selection of the best modern critical interpretations of Fanny Burney's novel, *Evelina*. The critical essays are reprinted here in the chronological order of their original publication. I am grateful to Jennifer Wagner for her erudition and judgment in helping me to edit this volume.

My introductory remarks take some exception to the feminist readings that are strongly represented in this book. Ronald Paulson begins the chronological sequence of criticism by comparing *Evelina* to Smollett's *Humphry Clinker*.

In Susan Staves's discussion, we are reminded of the difficulties of being a female as Evelina confronts them. Variations upon this argument are eloquently manifested by Patricia Meyer Spacks's analysis of the "dynamics of fear" in the novel, and by Judith Lowder Newton's view of *Evelina* as a "chronicle of assault."

Mary Poovey's feminist emphasis is upon the novel's reflection of Fanny Burney's "trauma" at growing up the daughter, rather than the son, of the celebrated Charles Burney, friend of Johnson, Edmund Burke, and Sir Joshua Reynolds.

This book concludes with two previously unpublished essays that provide refinements upon earlier feminist criticism. In a brief exegesis, Jennifer Wagner considers "privacy and anonymity" in *Evelina* as figurations for achieving "a name of one's own," while Julia Epstein charts the "sophisticated and knowing rebellion" of Evelina against the violence offered her in and by her society.

Introduction

Evelina or the History of a Young Lady's Entrance into the World (1778) earned the approbation of Dr. Samuel Johnson, who remains in my judgment, as in that of many others, the best critic in Western literary history. These days *Evelina* seems to attract mostly feminist critics, though it is hardly a precursor of their ideologies and sensibilities. A reader who knows the novels of Samuel Richardson will recognize immediately how indebted Fanny Burney was to him, and any reader of Jane Austen will be interested in *Evelina* in order to contrast the very different ways in which Richardson influenced the two women novelists. In itself, *Evelina* provides a rather mixed aesthetic experience upon rereading, at least to me. Its largest strength is in its humor and in Fanny Burney's quite extraordinary ear for modes of speech. What is rather disappointing is Evelina herself, who records the wit and spirits of others, while herself manifesting a steady goodness that is not ideally suited for fictional representation.

Entrance is indeed the novel's central metaphor, and Evelina enters the social world as a kind of lesser Sir Charles Grandison, rather than as a lesser Clarissa. This is not to say that Evelina's advent in the book does not please us. Fanny Burney shrewdly delays, and we do not have direct acquaintance with Evelina until the lively start of Letter 8:

> This house seems to be the house of joy; every face wears a smile, and a laugh is at every body's service. It is quite amusing to walk about and see the general confusion; a room leading to the garden is fitting up for Captain Mirvan's study. Lady Howard does not sit a moment in a place; Miss Mirvan is making caps; every body so busy!—such flying from room to room!—so many orders given, and retracted, and given again! nothing but hurry and perturbation.

1

Ronald Paulson praises *Evelina* as a careful balance of the old and the new, of Smollettian satire and a pre-Austenian ironic sensibility. I am surprised always when Smollett's effect upon Fanny Burney is judiciously demonstrated, as it certainly is by Paulson, precisely because Evelina cannot be visualized as journeying in the superbly irascible company of Matthew Bramble, whereas one can imagine her in dignified converse with Sir Charles Grandison. That seems another indication of a trouble in *Evelina* as a novel, the trouble alas being Evelina herself. In a world of roughness and wit, she remains the perpetual anomaly, too good for her context and too undivided to fascinate her reader. One implicit defense of Evelina is the polemic of Susan Staves, who views the heroine's dominant affect as being one of acute anxiety, since she is frequently in danger of sexual (or quasi-sexual) assault. Staves has a telling and lovely sentence: "Evelina's progress through the public places of London is about as tranquil as the progress of a fair-haired girl through modern Naples." Surrounded by Smollettian characters, the non-Smollettian Evelina must struggle incessantly to maintain her delicacy. That is clearly the case, and yet again, this creates a problem for the reader. Delicacy under assault is very difficult to represent except in a comic mode, since more of our imaginative sympathy is given to rambunctiousness than to virtue.

This makes it highly problematic, at least for me, to read *Evelina* either as a study in the dynamics of fear or as a chronicle of assault. If I find Evelina herself a touch too bland in her benignity, nevertheless she seems to me commendably tough, and rather less traumatized than some feminist critics take her to be. Historical changes in psychology are very real, and eighteenth-century men and women (of the same social class) have more in common with one another than say eighteenth-century women intellectuals have in common with our contemporary feminist critics. Evelina (and Fanny Burney) are less obsessed by Electra complexes, and less dismayed by female difficulties, than many among us, and a curious kind of anachronism is too frequently indulged these days.

Like her creator, Fanny Burney, who knew so well how to live in the forceful literary world of her father's companions, Evelina is ultimately stronger and shrewder than any of the men, and nearly all of the women, in her own universe. They may assault her delicacy, but she outwits them, and subtly triumphs over them. Her goodness does not exclude the skills of a grand manipulator. She is an anomaly in her sensibility, but not in her admirably poised social sense, and her manifold virtues coexist with an enigmatic cunning, suitable to the social psychology of her era.

Evelina: Cinderella and Society

Ronald Paulson

Fanny Burney's *Evelina* (1778), [one] critic [Montague and Martz] has observed, uses "*Humphry Clinker* as a base for operations in the direction of Jane Austen." Austen was a careful reader of Burney, and Burney owes an obvious debt to Smollett. Although the plot of *Evelina* receives a great deal more emphasis than that of *Humphry Clinker*, both novels are structurally a series of letters describing a series of places visited, an itinerary held together by a conventional sentimental plot. Unacknowledged fathers, the lowly who turn out to be highborn, and brothers who find their lost sisters are all ingredients of the sentimental plot in both novels. The themes in both—though different—are conveyed by the cities and country houses visited. Evelina goes from the country to London with the acceptable Mirvan family; then back to the country and again to London, this time in the company of the impossible, vulgar Branghtons and Mme. Duval; then back to the country and to Bristol Hot Well with people of quality, the Beaumonts; and finally to Bath with Lord Orville. The effect here is not too different from that of a scene in London or Bath seen through the eyes of Bramble, then Jery, and then Winifred Jenkins and Tabitha. In a more formalized, static way, these letters serve the function of Evelina's different guides, revealing and opposing "different points of view and incompatible ways of meeting the same experience" (Baker). In this sense *Humphry*

From *Satire and the Novel in Eighteenth-Century England.* © 1967 by Yale University. Yale University Press, 1967.

Clinker points away from the true-false world of formal verse satire toward the infinitely qualified world of the novel of manners.

The central unit of both novels is the test scene in which the attitudes of various types are brought together and analyzed. *Evelina* is a series of these big scenes—Evelina's first assembly, her first opera, the drawing room of the Beaumonts, and so on. In *Humphry Clinker* the moral discourse in which one satirist attacks an evil is the simplest scene of this sort: Bramble attacks the affectation that makes people desire the fashionable waters of Bath, however disgusting and unhealthy. There are also scenes in which more than one satirist appears, and the object of attack is not so clearly defined. As we move north, away from the blatant folly of London, these scenes increase in number and the distinctions between right and wrong become less clear-cut. The practical jokes and counter practical jokes of the Bulford house party, with their repercussions of hurt pride and endangered health, raise the question of who in a given circumstance is right and who is wrong. And what of Micklewhimmen, the sophisticate who pretends to be an invalid in order to excite compassion from the ladies? The alarm of fire being sounded, he proves himself both wholly sound and a coward, knocking down old ladies in his hurry to save himself; but his good-humored acceptance of the unmasking, ending in his dancing a jig, leaves one wondering whether he is admirable or not; whether he or Bramble or a clergyman who enters into the argument or Tabby, who refuses to forgive him under any circumstances, is really right. There are also the scenes in which Bramble, Lismahago, Tabby, and others argue, social types mix, manners are tested, and the norm of behavior becomes, almost inevitably, a compromise between two or more partially correct attitudes.

These scenes place the satirist in a larger context. Like Harriet Byron and Charlotte Grandison, Bramble is finally just one more point of view, one more example, in the larger picture of the novel. In *Evelina* Burney presents the characteristic satiric figures common in Smollett's novels—the sharp-tongued Mrs. Selwyn, the practical-satirist Captain Mirvan, and in his way even the fop Lovel. But in every case they are regarded coldly, the moral or public content has gone out of their observations, and they are merely private characters, their particular satiric approach a pattern of manners. Mirvan is a case in point; he is the Smollettian sea dog, as well as the prankster and the Juvenalian whose indignation bubbles over into violent action when confronted with such outrages to his native John Bullishness as the preposterous

Mme. Duval. He can be found in any of Smollett's novels, but he has undergone the same metamorphosis as Holder and Bulford in *Humphry Clinker;* he has become a prankster and a boor. The difference appears in the one scene in which Mirvan most resembles the early Smollettian satirists, Random, Pickle, and Cadwallader Crabtree—the incident in which he dresses up a monkey to look like the fop Lovel. The monkey is a commentary on Lovel just as the Pygmalion girl Peregrine creates is a commentary on high society, but the monkey proceeds to emphasize the cruelty beyond satire by biting Lovel's ear. The scene arouses only pity for Lovel, who for a moment becomes a human being as well as a fop. By contrast, the moral function is completely absent in all Mirvan's other pranks, and in the pranks he plays on Mme. Duval he appears simply as a coarse lout, like his counterparts in *Humphry Clinker.*

The chief difference between the two novels, however, lies in the fact that in *Evelina* the places and scenes not only are part of a satiric survey of society, but also are stages in the social climb of a young girl. One difficulty in Smollett's novels up to *Humphry Clinker* was his inability to merge his sentimental plot conventions and his real center of interest (the satiric scene); *Evelina* carries Smollett's work a step further, fitting his psychological form to the logical form of the courtship. For this aspect of her novel, Burney drew upon *Sir Charles Grandison,* omitting the melodramatic end of the spectrum. But the plot Burney follows in *Evelina* is not solely made up of the stages of a courtship; it simultaneously consists of the stages in the social ascent of a young girl. Evelina, the chief letter writer of the novel, has much in common with Harriet Byron, but she has more with Sir Charles Grandison's young ward, Emily Jervois, a naive observer without Harriet's certainty in her own judgment; Emily's horrible mother becomes Evelina's Mme. Duval, with the implications more fully developed.

Evelina is sharp and critical, and her standards are high; but as Bramble is isolated by his illness, she (like Humphry Clinker) is isolated by her birth. She is outside society, of obscure parentage, and comes from a sheltered life in the country which sets off the vice of London in vivid relief. However, the function of her equivocal position is no longer simply to make her a touchstone or a satirist (though she is a little of both) but to put her outside society—a "nobody" as Lovel calls her—so that she literally does not know who she is; her progression then is not, like Harriet's, toward fulfillment, but toward self-definition and identity.

The same progression is evident in both Bramble and that other "nobody" Humphry. Bramble is shown as a man in search of health, which is finally a knowledge of his own past, achieved by going back over the country of his youth and making an important discovery about himself. But in *Humphry Clinker* searches for self-definition are tangential and subordinate and thus are only other aspects of a larger theme dealing with attitudes toward experience in general. In *Evelina* the satiric aspects, the attitudes toward the world, are subordinated to the protagonist's personal search, which is thus the theme of the novel.

Although Evelina has the satirist's inclination, she is closer to the character of Lydia Melford. What Smollett did not see was the possibility of making the young girl with a finer sensibility than his masculine characters a satirist, perhaps because he knew she lacked the freedom of choice of a man and so could not finally maintain the satirist's standards. Lydia, the naive, impressionable, sensitive young girl, comes to each new place with wide eyes and (like her uncle and brother) is appalled at what she discovers; pretty soon, however, she recognizes the fashionableness of it and tries to adjust. Lydia is a rough sketch for the figure of a young girl like Evelina, who is an outsider, is sensitive enough to see the wrongness of the society she enters, but still knows she must make common cause with it; she must come to terms with a society she has first seen through.

The obvious source for this aspect of *Evelina,* however, is the French novelist Marivaux's *Vie de Marianne* (1731; Eng. trans., 1736). Burney takes not only the names Duval and Mirvan from Mme. Dutour and Mme. de Miran, and Orville from M. de Valville, but also the situation of the girl in the anomalous position of not knowing her parents but suspecting that they were noble and rich: "If my only Fault," she says, "had been not to be born of rich Parents; had I but a noble extraction without a Fortune; all still would have been safe." But she believes herself to be of a rich, noble family, while her actual status is not above a linen draper's. Her actions soon convince the reader of her quality, but society is not so ready to grant her the place she deserves. She has to bear the middle-class abuse of her linen–draper landlady, an attempted seduction by her "benefactor" M. de Climal, threatened poverty, the jealousy and interference of her potential husband's family, her lover's unfaithfulness, and finally, just when she is on the verge of success, the greedy clutches of the Church which would cheat her out of her recently acquired inheritance.

A brief contrast with *Joseph Andrews* is in order. Fielding may have looked to *Marianne* as a useful example of how Richardson *should* have written; here he found a similar plot (again perhaps one of Richardson's sources) but also detachment, analysis, and criticism of the protagonist as well as a broader and less intense view of experience. The single action of the attempted seduction, which takes up a large part of *Pamela,* is dispatched quickly in *Marianne.* When M. de Climal attempts to seduce Marianne he is scorned and dismissed; though she is left temporarily destitute, there is no danger that she will lose her honor. Instead of experiencing one, long, intense trial, Marianne is confronted by a variety of obstacles which bring her into contact with a cross section of French society, from country clerics to tradespeople, from convent nuns to vain young women and gossips. Fielding has Joseph suffer the same persecution and end a scion of a good family. His gentility also shows through as a natural virtue, evident to the perceptive.

The difference between Joseph and Marianne (or Evelina) is notable, however: he is given no awareness of his true status and so never aspires. There is no conflict within him, and his relationship with society is the simple satiric one of virtue persecuted. Fielding merely substitutes charity for chastity as Joseph's main motive force. On the other hand, Marianne (and much more, Jacob in Marivaux's *Paysan parvenu*) acts with a consummate sense of the realities that Joseph blithely ignores. Her virtues are social rather than personal, and her delicate sensibility expresses a happy blending of the ability to respond emotionally and an acuteness in judging the results of a generous and timely action.

In a sense Marivaux has in a single try hit upon the novel of manners that the English slowly evolved over another half-century through the gradual refining of satiric forms and intentions. The two basic situations of the novel of manners illustrate the point. The first is the situation that developed in England as the satirist-satirized was refined into a Dr. Primrose and an Evelina. At the beginning of part 2 of Marivaux's novel, Marianne goes to church and observes (as the first-person narrator) all the fashionable folk posing and posturing in their pews. She is a country girl in the great city, and she describes these manners with a fresh style, meditates a bit on them, and then tells how her own simplicity and beauty drew all eyes away from the affected coquettes. For just an instant she sets off the artificial beauty of the others by her own natural beauty, smiling at the psychology of the men (her hand, she says, is what captures them). But almost at once the reader's interest shifts from the coquettes and the beaux looking at Marianne to her own psychology: she is not merely a device for showing up the artifice of the coquettes; she is a character who is becoming vain talking about their vanity.

Her flaw has hardly been fastened upon when the situation is completely overturned by her seeing a handsome young man (Valville) and becoming herself enamored. This leads into the second situation, which could not have taken place with the innocence of Joseph Andrews—the scene of snobbery leading to embarrassment. Marianne has been so smitten by Valville that she walks in front of a horse on her way home and is saved by him. With her apparent gentility she soon has Valville's heart at least partly in her grasp. But only with much difficulty does she keep from him the nature of her lodgings with a linen draper. When the coach takes her from Valville's house to her lodgings, her landlady characteristically attacks the coachman as a highway robber who should be beaten rather than paid. Marianne is horrified to see her lover's footman across the street, taking in the whole, sordid, middle-class scene, which she has tried so hard to keep from Valville. (Significantly, the embarrassment is at the hands of Mme. Dutour, as Evelina's is at the hands of Mme. Duval.)

The scene of embarrassment is more particularly a testing. Embarrassment, for example, is only one of Marianne's reactions. Mme. Dutour exhibits behavior that can be painful only to refined sentiments. The crucial test of this sort comes with M. de Climal's proposition. Assuming that Marianne's virtue corresponds to her social position, he offers her a guaranteed yearly stipend for her consent. Her scornful refusal is a rejection of the moral position of an entire class and demonstrates convincingly her true affiliation with a higher class. Mme. Dutour's middle-class reaction (similar to the one Fielding attributed to Pamela) is to advise Marianne to play Climal for all he is worth—to accept his presents and then let him discover that his money will not buy her virtue. The two elements are constantly in tension—the girl's lack of social status and her actual possession of it. Thus Marianne and Evelina can be shown in scenes in which snobbery leads to embarrassment, in scenes in which embarrassment or indignation is justified (a revelation of their true affiliation with the upper classes), and often in scenes in which both appear simultaneously.

Evelina's struggles to keep the unpleasant Sir Clement Willoughby from seeing her with the Branghtons are very reminiscent of Marianne's efforts to keep Valville from learning where she lives. The important difference is that in the English novel of manners the emphasis is usually on the social blunder and thus on the satire rather than on the sensibility that naturally excludes such as the Branghtons, for Willoughby (unlike Valville), any sensible girl should know, has nothing to offer but his gentility. Even the scenes with the worthy Orville usually put the emphasis on Evelina's error. The novel of manners in England again reveals its derivation from the Quixotic anti-romance in which the aspiring knight in his hopelessly ill-fitting armor but noble heart goes after windmills; he is the ancestor of the girl who does not know her parents but, being a natural aristocrat, half-consciously aspires to social poise and the hand of an earl, committing terrible gaffes, some of which are unpardonable, along the way.

Evelina has too much of the Smollettian character in her to lose all traces of the satiric device. Her embarrassment—the effect of the Branghtons' faux pas on her delicate sensibility—can be taken as another mutation of Bramble's violent reaction to sociomoral corruptions. At any rate, the reactions of cultivated heroines in scenes with boors are gentle cousins to the satiric outburst. In *The Mysteries of Udolpho* Emily reacts thus to the vulgarity of Mme. Cheron: her "countenance, during this coarse speech, varied every instant, and towards its conclusion her distress had so much increased that she was on the point of leaving the room." The embarrassment of Evelina is more personal than Bramble's; her future with an aristocratic husband is at stake, and so, in the celebrated scene at the opera, her enlightened self-importance is caught in the same satiric situation as the Branghtons' stupid self-importance. Both roles are still distinct enough to make her derivation from the English satiric tradition plain, and yet they dramatically merge as they lead her toward abduction at the hands of the proper gentleman Willoughby.

Smollett always stops short of this treatment of the personal problem because, although he reduces his satirical spokesman's attitude to just one way of looking at the world, he still shares with his satirical forebears the assumption that the individual's quest is not as important as the many different endeavors of the people surrounding him. This may offer an explanation for the form of the anatomy he employs, where person after person and scene after scene receive varying but not disproportionate emphasis; the whole human organism is the important consideration, and the satirist feels that a hand or a foot should never make one lose sight of the larger meaning of the whole. In this sense *Evelina* is a careful balance of the old and new: the anatomy of society is still present, and the protagonist is still functioning as a satiric device, but the fictional form given these matters is about to absorb and subordinate them all to the single theme of the protagonist's growing self-awareness.

Evelina; or, Female Difficulties

Susan Staves

There is a remarkable degree of critical consensus on the merits of *Evelina*, Fanny Burney's popular novel. This consensus is for the most part sound, but it has one aspect which strikes me as peculiar. Descriptions of the novel make it appear to be a combination of the usual romance with cheerful, albeit occasionally malicious, satire. The primary criticism of the book is that it is hopelessly trivial. Yet Evelina's predominant emotion seems to me to be an acute anxiety which is painful, real, and powerful.

Traditional approaches to *Evelina* stress Fanny Burney's place in literary history as a transitional figure between the major novelists of the mid-eighteenth century and Jane Austen. Critics also seem to agree that her plots are perfunctory, simply "wood and wire" on which to hang the true attraction of her work, the humorous characters and delightful comic episodes. The plots, Macaulay wrote, "are rudely constructed and improbable, if we consider them in themselves. But they are admirably framed for the purpose of exhibiting striking groups of eccentric characters, each governed by his own peculiar whim, each talking his own peculiar jargon, and each bringing out by opposition the oddities of all the rest."

The most intriguing note repeatedly struck in the criticism, however, is the claim that *Evelina or the History of a Young Lady's Entrance into the World* is somehow a quintessentially feminine book.

From *Modern Philology* 73, no. 4, pt. 1 (May 1976). © 1976 by the University of Chicago.

It exhibits, we are told, the peculiar strengths and weaknesses of the feminine mind. On the one hand, there is a praiseworthy accuracy and minuteness in the observation of manners. On the other hand, the book's concerns are ultimately lacking in significance. Discussing Fanny Burney in his *Lectures on the Comic Writers,* Hazlitt offers a remarkable statement of this position:

> Women, in general, have a quicker perception of any oddity or singularity of character than men, and are more alive to every absurdity which arises from a violation of the rules of society, or a deviation from established custom. This partly arises from the restraints on their own behaviour, which turn their attention constantly on the subject. . . . They have less muscular strength; less power of continued voluntary attention—of reason, passion, and imagination: but they are more easily impressed with whatever appeals to their senses or habitual prejudices. . . .
>
> There is little other power in Miss Burney's novels, than that of immediate observation: her characters, whether of refinement or vulgarity, are equally superficial and confined. The whole is a question of form, whether that form is adhered to or infringed upon. It is this circumstance which takes away dignity and interest from her story and sentiments, and makes the one so teazing and tedious, and the other so insipid. The difficulties in which she involves her heroines are too much "Female Difficulties"; they are difficulties created out of nothing.

Writing in 1945, Lord David Cecil agreed with Hazlitt, "By nature, women are observers of those minutiae of manners in which the subtler social distinctions reveal themselves." Fanny Burney's "thinness" also was to him "symptomatic of a fundamental lack of mental distinction."

Hazlitt was undoubtedly right to feel that contemporary women were likely to be sensitive to social decorum because of the restraints on their own behavior, and right to say that the difficulties in which Fanny Burney involves her heroines are "Female Difficulties." In fact, her final novel, *The Wanderer,* uses that phrase as its subtitle. We may, though, disagree that such difficulties are created "out of nothing" and find it worthwhile to analyze exactly what they are. Such an analysis may also suggest a more vital relationship than has previously appeared between the much-abused plot of the novel and the incidental comedy.

We may notice immediately that Evelina's anxiety is partly provoked by physical violence and threats of violence. She is subjected to assaults which—though they could happen in Richardson—could not conceivably be made on heroines in Jane Austen or even in Dickens. When she tries to rescue her grandmother from a ditch, Madame Duval suddenly hits her "a violent slap on the face!" Returning from the opera, she is trapped alone with Sir Clement Willoughby in his coach. She tries to withdraw her hand from him, "but in vain, for he actually grasped it between both his, without any regard to my resistance." More and more terrified and certain Sir Clement has lied to her about ordering the coachman to drive her home, she makes "a sudden effort to open the chariot-door" to jump from the moving coach into the street. He catches hold of her, continuing his declaration of love until she puts her head out of the window and shouts. Sir Clement pursues Evelina throughout the novel, seizing her another time in Mrs. Beaumont's garden until she is released by Lord Orville. Shortly thereafter he tears the forged letter out of her hand, ripping it into "a thousand pieces" and catching hold of her gown to prevent her escape.

Evelina's progress through the public places of London is about as tranquil as the progress of a fair-haired girl through modern Naples. Every time she is accidentally separated from her protectors she is addressed with indelicate freedom, pursued, and usually grabbed. Walking with the Miss Branghtons down a long alley at Vauxhall, she encounters a rout of drunken men (she does not, of course, call them drunken):

> By the time we came near the end, a large party of gentlemen, apparently very riotous, and who were hallooing, leaning on one another, and laughing immoderately, seemed to rush suddenly from behind some trees, and, meeting us face to face, put their arms at their sides, and formed a kind of circle, which first stopped our proceeding, and then our retreating, for we were presently entirely enclosed. The Miss Branghtons screamed aloud, and I was frightened exceedingly; our screams were answered with bursts of laughter, and for some minutes we were kept prisoners, till at last one of them, rudely seizing hold of me, said I was a pretty little creature.

Evelina struggles to free herself from these men, only to run headlong into another group who treat her with equal roughness. Sir Clement appears to "rescue" her, but, putting the worst possible construction on her presence unescorted in the dark alleys of Vauxhall, he in his turn forces her to exert all her strength to push him away.

Some weeks later at Marybone Gardens Evelina is separated from her party when everyone is frightened by the fireworks accompanying a dramatization of the story of Orpheus and Eurydice. She seeks the others immediately, but "Every other moment I was spoken to by some bold and unfeeling man; to whom my distress, which I think must be very apparent, only furnished a pretence for impertinent witticisms, or free gallantry." Away from London in the quieter precincts of Bristol Hotwells, Evelina and Mrs. Selwyn nevertheless find their way along the Avon blocked by three rude men. On still another occasion, seeking safety in the company of two other young ladies, Evelina does not go "three yards" before being followed by yet another group of impertinent young men.

It must be acknowledged that Richardson's heroines suffer at least as much physical violence as Evelina does. In *Pamela, Clarissa,* and *Sir Charles Grandison* alike there is much pushing and shoving back and forth between the heroines and the men who would seduce them: Pamela and Clarissa are virtually imprisoned, Clarissa is raped, and Harriet Byron is abducted. In *Grandison*, the book that seems closest to *Evelina*, even the relatively mild Greville bruises Harriet. He snatches her hand, crying, "You shall give it to *me!*—and the strange wretch pressed it so hard to his mouth, that he made prints upon it with his teeth." During the extended episode of Sir Hargrave Pollexfen's abduction of Harriet, which resembles Sir Clement's briefer coach ride with Evelina, both Sir Hargrave and Harriet grow quite violent. She struggles and screams, dashes the prayer book from the Fleet parson's hands, and uses both her own hands to push away Sir Hargrave when he tries to kiss her "undefended neck." He hugs her, throws himself at her feet to embrace her knees "with his odious arms," and accidentally slams the door on her, giving her a bloody nose and bruising her stomach. Most memorably, he muffles her up in a cloak in the coach and forcibly stuffs a handkerchief in her mouth to prevent her screaming.

The effect of the assaults on Richardson's heroines, however, is quite different from the effect of the violence toward Evelina. For one thing, Richardson's heroines spend very little time in public places and so are not subjected to the pervasive anonymous violence Evelina encounters. More important, Harriet is twenty, and a much cooler, more poised woman who early establishes her superiority. Although she is, of course, physically weaker than Sir Hargrave, she is heroic enough to know that she will die rather than submit to him. Even in her fright, she has the presence of mind to reason with his underlings and to rebuke her enemies magisterially: "I adjure you, Sir," she says to the minister, "by that God in whose sight, you read, 'we are gathered together,' that you proceed no further. I adjure you, Sir Hargrave, in the same tremendous Name, that you stop further proceedings. My life take: With all my heart, take my life: But my hand, never, never, will I join with yours." The melodramatic language in which Harriet speaks and in which she describes the scenes distances us from the reality of a woman's terror. More self-conscious and more self-regarding than Evelina, Harriet also repeatedly heightens the pathos of her situation in the telling. "He had the cruelty," she complains, "to thrust a handkerchief in my mouth, so that I was almost strangled; and my mouth was hurt, and is still sore, with that and his former violence of the like nature."

Evelina's terrors seem more immediate and more real. The God who was a shield and bulwark to Richardson's heroines is outside of her awareness. Unlike Harriet, Evelina is also often partly responsible for her own distress and so must suffer the confusion of guilt. Most important, Evelina is usually too frightened to provide dignified condemnations or moral analyses of her persecutors' vices—or, indeed, to do much more than haltingly beg them to release her. Sir Clement is a strong and experienced man of thirty, Evelina a weak and naive girl of seventeen. Fanny Burney makes us feel that difference. When Evelina is alone in the coach with Sir Clement, he preserves his savoir faire while she is gradually reduced to stammering and speechlessness:

"For Heaven's sake, what is the matter?"

"I—I don't know," cried I (quite out of breath), "but I am sure the man goes wrong; and if you will not speak to him, I am determined I will get out myself."

"You amaze me" answered he (still holding me), "I cannot imagine what you apprehend. Surely you can have no doubts of my honour?"

He drew me towards him as he spoke. I was frightened dreadfully, and could hardly say, "No, Sir, no,—none at all: only Mrs. Mirvan,—I think she will be uneasy. . . ."

> Sir Clement, with great earnestness, endeavoured to ap-
> pease and compose me: "If you do not intend to murder
> me," cried I, "for mercy's, for pity's sake, let me get out!"

The disingenuous Sir Clement knows perfectly well that Evelina doubts
his honor, but he also calculates that she will be too embarrassed and
too terrified to admit it. Obviously she does not really think he is
interested in murdering her, yet her vocabulary can hardly include
terms directly descriptive of sexual assault and rape. Harriet has a
clearer notion of Sir Hargrave's intentions: first he will try to marry
her forcibly, then if he is made to despair of that purpose, he will
simply rape her and may or may not marry her afterward. Evelina
does not know exactly what Sir Clement wants to do to her. How
could she? Perhaps he only wants to declare his admiration, hold her
hand, and take her home. Perhaps her anxieties are those of a silly girl
who badly misjudges a worldly but honorable gentlemen. So Evelina
worries about being foolish as well as about the assaults which, to her,
remain terrifyingly nameless.

Evelina's anxiety, however, is more often provoked by psychic
threats than by the possibilities of physical assault. She worries constantly that her delicacy will be wounded or that it will appear to be
compromised. "Delicacy" seems to be a central concept in the novel
and is worth trying to define. As a positive virtue it arises from
awareness of the sensibilities and needs of others. Lord Orville, "the
most delicate of men," appreciates the potentialities for pain in various
situations and invents subtle ways of diminishing them. When Evelina
is separated from her friends after the opera, Sir Clement boldly offers
to take her with him in his coach, while Orville simply offers his coach
and servants, making it clear that he himself will go home in a chair.
Evelina is moved to exclaim, "How grateful did I feel for a proposal so
considerate, and made with so much delicacy!" After she has been seen
with the two whores at Marybone Gardens, Orville seeks to caution
her without suggesting that he suspects her virtue and without actually
saying that the women were whores. (Evelina in describing the women
to Mr. Villars in an early draft calls them "2 women of the Town"; in
the final version they become "two women of such character.") Mar-
veling at Orville's kindness on this occasion, Evelina cries, "How
delicate his whole behaviour! willing to advise, yet afraid to wound
me!"

True delicacy is opposed to cruelty, impertinence, and boldness; it is also superior to artificial decorums. False delicacy invokes lesser conventions to ignore the real needs of others. Orville, writes Mr. Villars, shows that he is above "a false and pretended delicacy" when he goes to Mrs. Mirvan's to secure Evelina's safety in the coach incident. Evelina would be guilty of false delicacy were she to shrink from entering Mr. Macartney's room as he is about to shoot himself. The Macartney episodes have generally been regarded as gratuitous; they do, however, give Evelina a chance to show that her delicacy is superior to mere convention and, since Macartney is impoverished and friendless, that she is not quite such an egregious snob as some critics would have us believe.

Delicacy becomes more problematic when we think of it as implying weakness and modesty or when we ask whether the same delicacy is being recommended for both sexes. Like many other eighteenth-century novels, *Evelina* sometimes seems to deny significant differences between its masculine ideal and its feminine ideal. Mr. Villars is pleased with Evelina's intrepidity in saving Mr. Macartney from suicide: "Though gentleness and modesty are the peculiar attributes of your sex, yet fortitude and firmness, when occasion demands them, are virtues as noble and as becoming in women as in men: the right line of conduct is the same for both sexes, though the manner in which it is pursued may somewhat vary, and be accommodated to the strength or weakness of the different travellers." Similarly, in *Cecilia* the heroine's refusal to collapse on the traumatic occasion of Mr. Harrel's suicide and her pragmatic exertions to ensure that the corpse is properly attended are offered as exemplary.

On the other hand, though, Fanny Burney sympathized with the general eighteenth-century desire to feminize the masculine ideal. Lord Orville is certainly being praised when, after Evelina's receipt of the forged letter, she laments, "I could have entrusted him with every thought of my heart . . . so steady did I think his honour, so *feminine* his delicacy." The boldness, activity, independence, and aggressive sexuality which had earlier been associated with masculinity were all objects of incessant attack. Propaganda against dueling was symptomatic and pervasive: it was criticized by Steele in *The Christian Hero,* attacked by Fielding's Dr. Harrison in *Amelia,* repeatedly preached against by Grandison, and numbered among George Primrose's sins by Sir William Thornhill. Orville is not known ever to have engaged in a duel; Edgar Mandelbert in *Camilla* rather seeks to prevent other men's duels than to fight his own; and even Mortimer Delvile, the only hero in Fanny Burney who does fight, repents his action immediately. Other late-eighteenth-century novelists went further still in forcing the renunciation of masculine aggressiveness and the assumption of modesty. In Henry Mackenzie's *The Man of Feeling*, the hero faints when the heroine confesses her love and then actually dies of the shock.

Nevertheless, female delicacy does have some discrete identity, and Fanny Burney regards it with the utmost seriousness. Many things which may be the proper object of a man's attention must be hidden from women. In the *Early Diary* we read of the strange gentleman who is forbidden Dr. Burney's tea table because he does not understand this and of the kind Mr. Rishton, who reads Spenser's *Faerie Queene* to Fanny and his wife, "in which he is extremely delicate, omitting whatever, to the poet's great disgrace, has crept in that is improper for a woman's ear." Of particular interest in *Evelina* is the early scene in which the heroine, Orville, Captain Mirvan, and their friends watch Congreve's *Love for Love*. Captain Mirvan proves an excellent critic of the drama, asserting, "it's one of the best comedies in our language, and has more wit in one scene than there is in all the new plays put together." Lord Orville, though later acknowledging that Congreve cannot be pleasing to the ladies, appears to like the play himself; during the performance he is observed to be "in excellent spirits, and exceedingly entertaining." (In his defense, it must be noted that it is undoubtedly the expurgated version of *Love for Love* prepared by Thomas Sheridan in 1776 which he sees.) Still, ladies of delicacy like Mrs. Mirvan and Evelina cannot enjoy themselves. They are obliged to be "perpetually out of countenance," and Evelina has to say that though the play "is fraught with wit and entertainment" she hopes never to see it again. Since even in the expurgated act 1 the hero Valentine is dunned for money for one of his bastards and visited at his lodgings by Mrs. Frail, it is not hard to discover offenses against female delicacy. Indeed, the heroine Angelica, though singled out by Orville as "the only female in the play worthy of being mentioned to the ladies," expresses sentiments and uses language which must have been shocking by late eighteenth-century standards. In her first appearance she teases her uncle Foresight, warning, "I can neither make you a cuckold, uncle, by going abroad; nor secure you from being one, by staying home."

Female delicacy can be wounded and, if wounded often enough or seriously enough, actually killed. Delicacy is in part like virginity:

once lost it cannot be regained. Yet it is still more fragile and precarious than virginity, since it can be eroded by the social ambiance in which one finds oneself. Dr. James Fordyce, in his famous *Sermons to Young Women*, paints in lurid colors the gradual death of modesty: "For a while they [young women] are shocked at signs of rudeness. Their ears are wounded by the language of vice: Oaths, imprecations, double meanings, every thing obscene fills them with disgust and horror. But custom soon begets familiarity; and familiarity produces indifference. The emotions of delicacy are less frequent, less strong. And now they seldom blush, although perhaps they often affect it . . . their minds are already debauched." Part of the romance of Fanny Burney's fiction is that though her heroines suffer repeated attacks on their modesty, the laws of a romance world keep them from becoming actually contaminated. The emancipated women like Mrs. Selwyn and Mrs. Arlbery, however, show the end result of the process Dr. Fordyce describes.

Evelina begins as a delicate young girl and seems to think her problem is principally that she will be thought to be indelicate, rather than that she will actually become so. After her error at the ridotto, for instance, she is "inexpressibly concerned" that Orville will think her "bold or impertinent." She writes to Mr. Villars that she could almost kill herself "for having given him the shadow of a reason for so shocking an idea." For a woman, though, being thought to be indelicate is a serious social reality, not something to be dismissed as mere appearance. Knowing how pure her nature is, Mr. Villars nevertheless cautions his ward against Sir Clement: "The slightest carelessness on your part will be taken advantage of by a man of his disposition." Assured safety lies only in obscurity and absolute punctiliousness; merely to frequent public places is to be exposed to risk. Dr. Fordyce offers the same warnings Mr. Villars does, making the dangers still more explicit:

> If a young person (supposing her dispositions in other respects ever so good) will be always breaking loose through each domestic inclosure, and ranging at large the wide common of the world, these destroyers . . . will consider her as lawful game, to be hunted down without hesitation. . . . With regard to the better sort of men . . . if in the flutter of too public a life you should at any time so far forget yourselves, as to drop that nice decorum of appearance and

> manner, which is expected from your sex . . . they will be
> tempted to harbour suspicions which I dare not name.

In *Evelina* the epistolary form makes Orville's possible suspicions a
subject of surmise, but in *Camilla*, where there is an omniscient narrator, Edgar Mandelbert's doubts about another pure heroine occasionally betrayed into the appearance of impropriety are carefully described.

Mr. Villars and Dr. Fordyce make the roots of Evelina's anxiety
clear: if she offends against the decorums of the ballroom by rejecting
one partner and then dancing with another, or if she is seen with the
vulgar Mr. Smith's hands on her shoulders, people will think that she
is a coquette lost to all true feminine feeling, a proper object of insult,
and if not physically, then mentally, promiscuous. "Is it enough for a
young woman to be free from imfamy, from crimes?" asks Dr.
Fordyce, "Between the state of pure virgin purity and actual prostitu-
tion are there no intermediate degrees? Is it nothing to have a soul
deflowered?" The slighest breach of decorum subjects Evelina to being
thought a lost woman; men's liberties with her will be justified, she
will be in greater danger of rape, and, of course, no Lord Orvilles or
Edgar Mandelberts will want to marry her. Hazlitt's complaint that
Fanny Burney centers on the question of whether forms are adhered to
or infringed upon is fair enough as a description, but the forms
themselves are by no means trivial; they have the gravest implications
for the women characters. Significantly, at least one contemporary
reviewer who was fond of *Evelina* seems to have considered the heroine's breaches of decorum as equivalent to Tom Jones's drunkenness,
whoring, fighting, and being kept by Lady Bellaston. In the *Critical
Review* of 1788 he longs "to see a female character drawn with faults
and virtues, to see her feel the effects of misconduct, which does not
proceed from a bad heart or a corrupted inclination, . . . in short to see
a female Jones, or another Evelina, with faults equally embarrassing,
yet as venial." As Mr. Villars wrote, "Nothing is so delicate as the
reputation of a woman; it is at once the most beautiful and most brittle
of all human things."

Evelina's fears are objectified when, to her "inexpressible horror,"
she finds herself walking arm in arm with the whores in Marybone
Gardens. Escaping from a young officer, she darts unsuspecting to
seek their protection. Lord Orville passes once without noticing her,
and then a second time, seeing her, almost causing her to faint, "so
great was my emotion, from shame, vexation, and a thousand other

feelings, for which I have no expressions." Contact between the pure maiden and fallen woman is, in fact, nearly an obligatory scene in certain kinds of eighteenth-century novels. Trapped for weeks in Mrs. Sinclair's brothel, Clarissa is also visited at Hampstead by Bab Wallis and Johanette Golding, whores Lovelace has coached to impersonate his relations; Sophia and Olivia Primrose are invited to come to live with Lady Blarney and Carolina Wilelmina Amelia Skeggs; Emily St. Aubert distinguishes female voices mingling with the brutal laughter of Montoni's confederates and is appalled to learn that Signora Livona, whose manners had so charmed her at Venice, now appears at Udolpho as her persecutor's mistress. The whores Evelina meets remain nameless and appear only briefly, but her fear of being confused with them is vivid and immediate.

Although Fanny Burney's romance plot has generally been considered a rather adventitious element of her novel, the importance of delicacy lends interest to her choice of the sensationalistic cliché of a clandestine marriage. How can a girl who is supposed to be a bastard establish herself as a young lady of delicacy? It is really inconceivable that a Harriet Byron or an Elinor Dashwood should have such sordid origins. For Richardson's taste, even the idea of a young man who was a bastard was hopelessly vulgar. Probably the only strictly delicate course open to Evelina—if there are any delicate courses open to female bastards—would be to remain in retirement with Mr. Villars and to die unmarried. Certainly it takes the very indelicate boldness of Madame Duval and Mrs. Selwyn to bring about her legitimization by Sir John Belmont.

But the special circumstances of Evelina's birth do have several functions. First, though proper young women were expected to remain almost entirely within their own domestic circles, the controversy over Evelina's legitimacy serves to force and to justify her contact with a much wider society. Like Juliet Granville in *The Wanderer* she is required by a sense of duty to forsake the protection of her genteel guardian; she does not improperly seek experience for experience's sake. Then, as is also true for Juliet, Evelina's birth leaves her particularly vulnerable to the physical and psychological threats to which women generally were subjected and, therefore, exposes those threats with great clarity. Finally, her origin is in itself an additional threat to delicacy, one which allows Madame Duval to terrify Evelina just as thoroughly as the strange men at Vauxhall do. When Madame Duval announces the scheme to resort to law to claim her granddaughter's birthright, Evelina is speechless with "surprise and terror." Like Clarissa, who will not litigate with her father for her estate and who will not prosecute Lovelace for rape, she recoils at the impiety of accusing her father, at the scandal of reviving her mother's story, and simply at appearing publicly in a law court. Mr. Villars immediately stigmatizes the plan as "violent, . . . public, . . . totally repugnant to all female delicacy."

The real tension in *Evelina* lies between the heroine's struggle to preserve her delicacy under these extraordinarily difficult conditions and the multitude of comic characters who constantly threaten it. These characters are not incidental to the romance plot; they are blocking characters with a closer relationship to the romance heroine than is usual. Madame Duval, Captain Mirvan, the Branghtons, and the others achieve their full comic effect because they are projections of Evelina's anxieties. They actually commit all the solecisms she is afraid of committing or of being thought to have committed. They are vulgar; they are immodest; they are ignorant of social decorums; they are openly satirical and contemptuous. Incident after incident is generated by an arrangement of circumstances which make it appear that Evelina is guilty of some indelicacy and therefore simply another member of the group of comic characters. At the performance of *Love for Love* Mr. Lovel makes the threat explicit by suggesting that there is not much difference between Evelina and Miss Prue.

As long as Evelina is alone with the vulgar characters she is able to observe their antics with some amusement and only occasional irritation. She can dissociate herself in her own mind from the Branghtons by branding their behavior as rude, pretentious, and unfeeling, whether the world thinks of them as her connections or not. Even if the vulgar Mr. Smith does conspire with Madame Duval to force her into the impropriety of accepting tickets to the ball from him, she can establish her mental superiority by sarcasms to Mr. Villars at his "elegant speech." But as soon as her association with such characters threatens to become known to a member of polite society, she becomes genuinely anxious. Letter 54, for example, reports with horrible fascination the words and deeds of Madame Duval and the Branghtons as they work their way to asking for Lord Orville's coach in Evelina's name. The passage attains its effect not so much through Evelina's protestations of "dread" and "agony" as by suspense built through such painfully minute recording of the characteristic remarks of her persecutors as their obtuseness tramples down her refinement. So "frantic" is

Evelina at their success that, like someone thrashing about in quicksand, she herself becomes guilty of the probable impropriety of writing an apologetic letter to Lord Orville.

The most interesting comic characters who function as projections of Evelina's fears are Captain Mirvan and Mrs. Selwyn. An analysis of their relation to her leads to some insights into the relationship between Evelina and Fanny Burney and into the consequences of eighteenth-century ideas about delicacy for Fanny Burney as an artist. In the *Early Diary* we discover a Miss Burney who is more boisterous, more ironic, and more sympathetic to laughter than the decorous Evelina, though certainly not without her own worries about delicacy. At Chessington, she describes the *Treatise upon Politeness* she promised to Miss Simmons, Mrs. Moore, and Kitty: "All this was taken as it was said, in sport, and we had much laughing in consequence of my scheme, which I accompanied by a thousand flighty speeches and *capricios*, for you know what my spirits are at . . . Chessington." The book, to be dedicated to Miss Notable of Swift's *Polite Conversation*, will be severe upon indelicate noises like coughing and laughing:

"Not to *cough?*" exclaimed every one at once; "but how are you to help it?"

"As to *that*," answered I, "I am not very clear about it myself, as I own I am sometimes guilty of doing it; but it is as much a mark of ill breeding, as it is to *laugh*; which is a thing that Lord Chesterfield has stigmatized." . . .

"And pray," said Mr. Crisp, making a fine affected face, "may you *simper?*"

"You may *smile* Sir," answered I; "but to *laugh* is quite abominable; though not so bad as *sneezing*, or *blowing the nose.*" . . .

"But pray, is it permitted," said Mr. Crisp, very dryly, "to *breathe?*"

"*That* is not yet, I believe, quite exploded," answered I; "but I shall be more exact about it in my book of which I shall send *you six* copies. I shall only tell you in general, that whatever is natural, plain, or easy, is entirely banished from polite circles."

Another episode in the *Diary* shows Fanny Burney seriously concerned about delicacy, but enjoying an atmosphere markedly less stuffy than anything with which Evelina or such later heroines as Fanny Price could feel comfortable. With Miss Allen and Miss Barsanti, she works to present scenes from Cibber's *The Careless Husband* at Mr. Crisp's house. Cibber was still more refined than the expurgated Congreve, but even his sentimental drama contains "a few exceptionable speeches" which Fanny Burney, playing Lady Graveairs, insists on omitting. In the days before the Evangelical piety which pervades the atmosphere of *Mansfield Park*, Mr. Crisp does not have any objections to private theatricals. Fanny Burney's stepsister, Miss Allen, goes so far as to borrow an entire suit of dark blue velvet from one Mr. Featherstone for her role as Sir Charles Easy. (Readers of Charlotte Brontë's *Villette* will recall that Lucy Snow, impressed into performing a male role in a school threatrical, refuses to injure female delicacy by wearing pants.) Miss Allen's appearance in the ill-fitting men's clothes raises outrageous mirth, provoking the admirable Mr. Crisp to "hollowing." Both Miss Austen and Miss Brontë would perhaps find it significant that Miss Allen later disgraced her family by engaging in a clandestine correspondence, marrying secretly at Ypres, and finally separating from her husband.

The more demure, more anxious regions of Fanny Burney's consciousness were appropriate to the character of a young lady heroine, but the lively, critical spirit of a satirist, which society and the marriage market found unappealing in young ladies, she disowns in the novel, splitting it off into figures like Captain Mirvan and Mrs. Selwyn. Though eighteenth-century readers tended to single out the Captain as the one unacceptably coarse note in an otherwise satisfactory novel, the author contrives to offer some support for his point of view. The saintly Mr. Villars confesses, "Shall I own to you, that, however I may differ from Captain Mirvan in other respects, yet my opinion of the town, its manners, inhabitants, and diversions is much upon a level with his own?" Like Congreve's Ben, to whom he is compared, the Captain is a brave and essentially good-hearted man; he exposes sham and administers his corporal punishments only to those who deserve them. Fanny Burney must have enjoyed inventing his monkey parody of Mr. Lovel, which concludes the novel, though upon the entrance of the monkey "full-dressed, and extravagantly *à la mode*," a meeker Evelina jumps up on the seat of her chair. At her first ball Evelina had struggled unsuccessfully with her laughter. When Lovel advanced to her and Orville, she interrupted his speech with laughing at his "stately foppishness," blushed for her folly, and actually caused the polite peer to stare. Now she knows better. Loud laughter belongs to the drunken men at Vauxhall and to the whores in Marybone Gardens.

The most articulate satirist is Mrs. Selwyn, who along with the Captain, Lord Merton, and Mr. Coverley, bursts into "a loud, immoderate, ungovernable fit of laughter" at the sight of the monkey. Fanny Burney sometimes uses Mrs. Selwyn as a satiric spokeswoman but preserves Evelina's respectability and her own by criticizing her freedom. Like Orville, but with a boldness allegedly objectionable in women, Mrs. Selwyn takes it upon herself to rebuke Evelina's persecutors. Affected by jealousy, Orville watches from a distance "with earnestness" while Lord Merton tries to make love to Evelina; Mrs. Selwyn advances to demand her release. Lovel, now Lady Louisa's sycophant, complains that Coverley has slighted her and committed "an outrageous solecism" in implying that Evelina is the best young woman there. Mrs. Selwyn retorts, "And pray, Sir, under what denomination may your own speech pass?" We are nevertheless encouraged to feel that Mrs. Selwyn has been placed by Evelina's characterization of her manners as "masculine," Mr. Villars's disgust at "her unmerciful propensity to satire," and even by the bad baronet's declaration that, "she has wit . . . and more understanding than half her sex put together; but she keeps alive a perpetual expectation of satire, that spreads a general uneasiness among all who are in her presence."

In fact, Mrs. Selwyn could almost be a character in Dr. Fordyce's *Sermons.* "A masculine woman," he advises, "must be naturally an unamiable creature. . . . To the men an Amazon never fails to be forbidding." The culture generally was severe on outspoken, learned, or masculine ladies, and characters like Mrs. Atkinson in *Amelia* and Miss Barnevelt in *Grandison* were also contrasted with more modest heroines and criticized for their pedantry or freedom. In ordinary life Fanny Burney seems to have shared this distaste, disapproving, for example, of the twenty-six-year-old Miss Bowdler, who was innocent, "very sensible and clever," but possessed of wit which spared "neither friend nor foe" and guilty of openly preferring the company of men.

All the resources of Fanny Burney's art are used to exorcise from Evelina and Lord Orville those qualities which give life to the book and to embody them in characters who are then criticized for their boldness. Even the revisions of this first published novel show her struggling to make the sympathetic characters use increasingly dignified language—striving, ironically, for the imitation Johnsonese of

Camilla, which almost all readers have deplored. Lord Orville must "fatigue himself" instead of "wear himself out"; Evelina must say, "I was so much disconcerted at this sneering speech that I said not a word" instead of "I was so mad at this sneering speech that I had hardly patience to make any reply." The later novels do not allow their young heroines to present their stories without the mediation of a narrator. So long as Fanny Burney had her anonymity, she could feel comfortable with simply criticizing the comic characters who failed to approach the standards of delicacy set by the humorless hero and heroine she endorsed. But, as Joyce Hemlow has suggested, when that anonymity was lost after the publication of *Evelina*, Miss Burney inevitably became still more inhabited: "I should certainly have been more finical, had I foreseen what happened," she declared: "I would rather a thousand times forfeit my character as a writer, than risk ridicule or censure as a female."

What, finally, are the female difficulties which are a subject of *Evelina*? First, there are the physical limitations which make women too weak to resist men who grab them and even too slow to run away. Then, there are the psychological restraints which force real and pretended ignorance about subjects from sexuality to money. Lord Orville wants to tell Evelina about the marriage settlements, but like all her sisters in the family of heroines, she assures him she is "almost ignorant of the word." Violations of the code of female delicacy, however minor, lead to anxiety that a woman will become a sort of outlaw who has lost her claim to the protection of society, protection which young women desperately need. Of course, many of Evelina's embarrassments seem all too familar to anyone, male or female, who has memories of a sensitive adolescence. Indeed, many female difficulties were rapidly becoming human difficulties as the passivity and modesty here required of Evelina were shortly to be required of the romantic heroes of Scott and Cooper. Nevertheless, the special vulnerability of a young woman in traditional society gives her anxieties a sharper edge.

Evelina tells and shows how difficult it is to be a young lady. With the sincerest desire for correctness, the heroine is forced into situations where she must offend punctilio. Her own grandmother orders her to accept ball tickets from a vulgar young man she barely knows. Her supposedly wise guardian abandons her to the authority of such a woman—and then warns that Madame Duval's judgment is poor and her associates of a kind likely to compromise Evelina. Beginning to know the world, Evelina reflects bitterly, "But I knew not, till now, how requisite are birth and fortune to the attainment of respect and civility." In short, much of the novel dwells upon the special helplessness of women to determine their own fates.

Yet the romance plot attempts to deny these novelistic truths. Lord Orville, "almost as romantic as if he had been born and bred at Berry Hill," refuses to draw the terrible inferences Evelina fears and, ignoring prudence, forgets to make his inquiries into Evelina's mysterious origins before declaring his love. *Cecilia, Camilla,* and *The Wanderer* similarly allow their heroines to be compromised in the eyes of their mentor heroes and then proceed to dissolve the serious complications in favor of romance conclusions. Many good, popular novels use this formula. Consciously and with philosophical sophistication, Fielding allows *Tom Jones* to rest on comparable contradictions; Smollett, too, denies the harshness of his picaresque tale at the end of *Roderick Random* when the hero is allowed to discover his beneficent and wealthy father in South America. *Pride and Prejudice* devotes much effort to teaching Elizabeth that the conditions of the marriage market are stern and that her imperfect relatives are significant facts about herself in the social world, then ends by letting her marry Darcy anyway. In *A Tale of Two Cities* a bleak view of human motives and abilities in the large social world is combined with the central romance of Lucie Manette and Charles Darney, creatures of magical simplicity and goodness. In the case of *Evelina,* the imposition of romance does not seem fully satisfying. The dichotomy between romance and realism is not acknowledged clearly, as it is in Fielding. We seem to be invited to accept the romance as a solution to evils for which Fanny Burney knows she does not really have a remedy. As Mr. Tyrold says more frankly in *Camilla,* "The proper education of a female" is "still a problem beyond human solution." The possibility of romance is present from the beginning in *Evelina,* as it is not in the early picaresque adventures of Roderick Random. Still, just as modern readers find it difficult to share Roderick's assumption that the world owes him specially favorable treatment because he has been born a gentleman, so it is hard to see just why Fanny Burney's heroines should receive the careful deference they seem to think is their due. Juliet Granville is certainly more irritatingly conscious of the deserts conferred upon her by her birth than Evelina is, but even Evelina seems a trifle huffy, especially when on the demotion of "poor Polly Green," the genteelly educated "bantling of Dame Green, wash-woman and wet nurse," she reports without comment and without comparison with her own fate Mrs. Green's feeling that the match with Mr. Macartney, though "inadequate to the pretensions of *Miss Belmont*," was "far superior to those *her daughter* could form after the discovery of her birth." Fanny Burney's notions of propriety would seem to leave open to criticism ladies who make friends of strangers not properly introduced and not properly connected, yet when her own heroines whose connections are not impeccable are coolly received, she endorses their grievances.

It is the novelistic truths in *Evelina* which seem especially worthwhile, the faithful rendering of recognizable experiences which are nowhere to be found in Richardson, Fielding, or Smollett. As good as the descriptions of manners are, as precisely as she catches the obnoxious Branghtons and the enervated Lady Louisa, Fanny Burney's exploration of Evelina's own embarrassments and anxieties is still more vivid and more valuable. Yet she could not finally deny the self-abnegation society required of ladies, and so, in rejecting the laughter, the irony, the satire, and the spirit of criticism, which seem to have been her natural gifts, she ultimately weakened her art.

Dynamics of Fear: Fanny Burney

Patricia Meyer Spacks

As novelist and as writer about herself, Fanny Burney takes a position in every respect opposed to Laurence Sterne. Committed to propriety as he to its opposite, apparently unaware of the formal possibilities or implications of her conventional plots, feeling that the most important question about novels concerned their moral influence, she reminds the reader that Tristram Shandy's conviction of the impossibilities of art does not represent the only conceivable viewpoint. The moral and psychological organization of her fiction and her diaries insists on the order of life itself. Keeping an intermittent record of herself for more than seventy years, she reveals not the chaos of experience but the reiteration of pattern. The rational structure of her prose helps her to assert the significant structure of her life.

A woman's vision? It seems important to say so. *Tristram Shandy* is organized to reveal the pervasiveness of male fear, demonstrating in form and in substance how the terror of impotence spreads through every endeavor. The entire mass of Fanny Burney's writing forms itself as centrally in relation to female fear—not of the absence of power but of failure of goodness and consequent loss of love. Tristram's fears reduce his life to disorder; Miss Burney's (and her heroines') have ordering force, defending against chaotic possibility.

Unique in her century in having left to posterity both a group of novels and the rich private record of voluminous letters and diaries,

From *Imagining a Self.* © 1976 by the President and Fellows of Harvard College. Harvard University Press, 1976.

Miss Burney also provides through her published work a basis for investigating the relationship between avowedly autobiographical and purportedly fictional accounts of experience. Previous critics have perceived this as a rather simple issue in her writing. Thus Ernest Baker writes: "Fanny Burney's importance in the history of the novel is . . . that she came so near to what may be called a direct transcript of life . . . There is only, as it were, a narrow and vanishing margin between literature and life. Scores of pages in her diaries may be put side by side with pages from her novels to illustrate this." Edwine Montague and Louis L. Martz comment about *Evelina:* "People who enjoy the *Diary* enjoy finding Fanny Burney in the novel too; and so the book becomes a kind of appendix to the *Diary.*" But neither novels nor diaries in fact offer anything like a "direct transcript." Both demonstrate the shaping of experience by a special sensibility, the artistry of pattern almost as manifest in letters and journals as in fiction. The pattern of Fanny Burney's life as she perceives and interprets it resembles the structures that shape her fictions, both converting psychological defense into literary tactics.

The two volumes of Fanny Burney's early diary, the six volumes first edited by her niece Charlotte Barrett, and the four volumes that have thus far emerged under Joyce Hemlow's editorship comprise an enormous mass of disparate material. They record public as well as private events: Miss Burney lived at Court for five years as Second Keeper of the Robes to Queen Charlotte; her subsequent marriage to a French emigré involved her at least peripherally in post-Revolution French politics. They demonstrate the literary and personal virtues with which their author has always been credited: her sharp ear for speech rhythms, her eyes for social detail, her sensitivity to manners as an index of moral quality, her devotion to her family, and her extreme propriety. The interpretative structure that forms her account of her life's happenings depends upon strategies of concealment. The idea of virtue provided Fanny Burney—as it has many women—a first line of defense. Goodness has always been a source of female force, a guard against enemies without and within. Miss Burney, hiding behind her impeccable morality, protects her inner life.

Two episodes reported at different times of her life exemplify Fanny Burney's characteristic moral stance. Writing of her beloved husband's death, which took place in 1819 (she was sixty-seven years old), she dwells in retrospect on her inner conflict over whether she would invite the priest to return after a single visit to the dying man's bedside. (D'Arblay, bred a Catholic, had preserved only a nominal allegiance to his church during his English residence. His wife, motivated by a sense of fitness, called a priest to administer the last rites.) She summarizes the dimensions of her psychic struggle: "The fear of doing wrong has been always the leading principle of my internal guidance." (In this instance, she adds, she finds herself "overpowered" by her inability to decide what was right and consequently unable to resolve on any course of action at all.) More than thirty years before, while she was still at Court, she had talked with the Reverend Charles de Guiffardière (always referred to in her journal as "Mr. Turbulent") about good conduct. He inquires whether she has ever done something she repents. Sometimes, she replies, but not often, "for it is not very often that I have done anything." What has saved her from misbehavior? Mr. Turbulent suggests prejudice, education, and accident. Miss Burney agrees, but adds *fear*. "I run no risks that I can see—I run—but it is always away from all danger that I perceive." Surely, Mr. Turbulent exclaims, such is not the "rule of right." Once more his interlocutor agrees, concluding the discussion, rather smugly, "I must be content that it is certainly not the rule of wrong."

Both these encounters, in addition to their psychological interest, suggest the literary possibilities of Miss Burney's principle of self-interpretation, an essentially dramatic view of her experience because it involves imagining goodness as precariously won and preserved and constantly to be defended, rather than as an achieved state of being. The active consciousness of danger that Fanny Burney reports emphasizes the potential drama within her quiet life, despite the fact that, as she confesses, she actually does little. Indeed, her refrainings themselves partake of her drama.

Reading the mass of the journals, one gradually realizes the energy of the decorous woman's verbal self-presentation, structured by her determination to be perceived as good, and her fear of negative judgment. The action of Fanny Burney's vast collections of journals and letters, like that of most women's writing in her century, derives from her attempt to defend—not to discover, define, or assert—the self. Both her choices and her ways of describing them testify to her productive and self-protective solution to unescapable problems of women's existence. That solution provides psychic space for her imaginative life, thus making her literary career possible, and also shapes the operations of her imagination.

The relation between Fanny Burney's loudly proclaimed concern with virtue and her impulse to write was an early theme of her diaries. Virtue and writing, it seemed in her youth, made utterly opposed demands. At the age of fifteen, she consigned to a bonfire all her literary production to date. Almost fifty years later, she explained why. "So early was I impressed myself with ideas that fastened degradation to this class of composition [fiction], that at the age of adolescence, I struggled against the propensity which, even in childhood, even from the moment I could hold a pen, had impelled me into its toils; and on my fifteenth birth-day, I made so resolute a conquest over an inclination at which I blushed, and that I had always kept secret, that I committed to the flames whatever, up to that moment, I had committed to paper." She sounds as though she is reporting a struggle against sexual sin ("propensity," "its toils," "an inclination at which I blushed," "secret") and the language of battle in which she records her suppression echoes the vocabulary in which her fiction relates her heroines' conflicts between reason and passion ("struggled against," "so resolute a conquest"). Writing fiction seemed to her, at the beginning, a fatal self-indulgence and writing fact, only slightly less menacing. Her friend Miss Young warns her that keeping a journal "is the most dangerous employment young persons can have—that it makes them often record things which ought *not* to be recorded, but instantly forgot." A few pages earlier, the diarist has inadvertently exposed two other hazards of her literary occupation: keeping a diary encourages a hunger for fresh experience, and it fosters undue reflectiveness about the experience one has. Miss Burney feels apologetic about her literary activity; she spends the morning on needlework, thus proving herself a good little woman, in order to justify an afternoon of reading and writing. But although she has burned her youthful novel, she continues her journalizing: a necessity of her psychic life.

In a letter to her "Daddy" Crisp, one of the older men who played important roles in her life partly as guardians of morality, Fanny, granting the "*general* superiority" of men to women, concludes that women's weakness stems from defects of head rather than heart. Women, therefore, must trust their emotions: hence, presumably, Fanny Burney's own adherence to fear as a sufficient guide to conduct. Yet they must also recognize the danger of their feelings. "Talking of happiness and misery, sensibility and a total want of feeling, my mama [i.e., her stepmother] said, turning to me, 'Here's a girl will *never* be happy! *Never* while she lives!—for she possesses perhaps as feeling a heart as ever girl had!' " To write a novel, Fanny believes as a girl, is to venture into dangerous realms of feeling and fantasy. To write a journal, on the other hand, may provide a way to deal with feelings as well as to express them. In the *Early Diary*, written for "nobody" (this strategy itself a youthful instance of the writer's defensive self-deprecation), we see the author struggling with moral and emotional dilemmas, using language to construct her defenses. The later journals, composed for various members of her family, show the process at a more advanced stage: writing now a means of consolidating and proclaiming already established defense systems. By the end of the *Early Diary*, Fanny Burney has rejected her first suitor, declaring her intent to live single. No further suitor presented himself, as far as we are told, until the man she accepted. She had defined clear channels for her emotional life.

Fear provided partial solutions for the crucial problem of a woman's relations with others. Twenty-one-year old Fanny mentally questions the conduct of Miss Bowdler, who "lives exactly as she pleases"; she concludes her account, "I can by no means approve so great a contempt of public opinion." Two years earlier, Fanny had encountered another young woman, a Miss Allen, who seemed to her possibly "too sincere: she pays too little regard to the world." The observer cannot decide what to think of such a phenomenon. She disapproves of the woman's ready disdain for "*harmless* folly," but she recognizes how "infinitely tiresome" such folly can seem and applauds the honesty of openly acknowledging the fact.

These two sets of observations sketch the issues of social relations as Fanny Burney understood them. Suffering from the impingement of conventional pressures on individual lives, she yearned for freedom. Yet convention, she understood, guarded feelings. The individual who boldly expressed her personal preferences (like Miss Bowdler's for men) or distastes (like Miss Allen's intolerance for folly) might hurt or mislead others. Despite Miss Burney's half-articulated desire to control her own destiny, she could not finally approve "contempt for public opinion." Manners and morals—as her four novels were to testify—reflected one another, in her conviction; the minutiae of socially acceptable conduct provided orthodox means for expressing consideration and concern for others. Fear of offending supplied a more potent principle of action than distaste for being offended.

As Fanny Burney discovered more and more emphatically the uses of fear as a principle of guidance in her life, she found also the way to tell her own story and came to understand the nature of the story she was constructing. "The act of journalizing," a theorist of autobiography writes, "intensifies the conflict in any autobiographer between life and pattern, movement and stasis, identification and definition, world and self." The observation applies hardly at all to Miss Burney as journalizer. Writing down her experience, she seems, on the contrary, to resolve potential conflicts between life and pattern and world and self. Discovering the structures of her life, she finds out how to feel about the world. As a result she contradicts also, essentially if not technically, the common generalization that, however highly wrought its individual entries, a "diary or journal as a complete work will never reflect the conscious shaping of a whole life for one informing purpose." One can speculate about how conscious the diarist's structuring could have been, but the sense of an informing purpose shaping her existence in the living and in the recording becomes increasingly strong. That purpose—to defend the freedom of the self by asserting fear of wrongdoing and commitment to virtue—involved familial, social, and literary relations, dictated action and restraint, and resolved as well as created conflict.

Often, particularly in Miss Burney's adolescence, the desire for freedom appeared to clash with the need to avoid offending. The conflict between the two dominates her *Early Diaries*.

> O! how I hate this vile custom which obliges us to make slaves of ourselves!—to sell the most precious property we boast, our time;—and to sacrifice it to every prattling impertinent who chooses to demand it!—Yet those who shall pretend to defy this irksome confinement of our happiness, must stand accused of incivility,—breach of manners—love of originality,—and . . . what not. But, nevertheless . . . they who will nobly dare to be above submitting to chains their reason disapproves, them shall I always honour—if that will be of any service to them! For why should we not be permitted to be masters of our time?—Why may we not venture to love, and to dislike—and why, if we do, may we not give to those we love the richest jewel we own, our time?

Miss Burney's sequences of reflection, in those early years, repeatedly duplicate the structure of this passage. The strong impulse to reject custom's slavery wavers in the face of anticipated charges of incivility. When the impulse returns to dominance, it has changed form: the author no longer imagines defying convention herself, only honoring those brave enough to do so, with an edge of self-contempt for her own ineffectuality. She can conclude her consideration only in unanswerable questions that express her resentment of the course of conformity she has chosen. Similarly, we find her meditating on love, confessing that she wishes "truly, really, and greatly . . . to be *in love*" and committed to a feeling devoid of rational justification, self-sufficient and satisfying. But soon she condemns such a longing as "foolish and ill-judged!" explaining that she does not really know what she says, she cannot mean it. Feeling leads in opposite directions.

When Mr. Barlow proposes to Fanny, that point becomes painfully apparent. She has long associated marriage with lack of freedom. The prospect of her own marriage reduces her to panic. Manifestly admirable though Thomas Barlow is, her heart tells her that she cannot unite herself with him. Her revered father and her "Daddy" Crisp argue his case; her deep desire always to comply with their wishes wars with her disinclination to marry. She thinks about "the duty of a wife": how hard it must be, "practised without high esteem!" Her reluctance, it seems, is sexual. But she continues, "And I am too spoilt by such men as my father and Mr. Crisp to content myself with a character merely inoffensive." She prefers a father to a husband. Her father, opposing male reason to female emotion, urges serious consideration of Barlow's suit. Fanny, realizing that reason offers her no support, creates a lavish display of emotion, unable to eat, constantly weeping, feeling more misery than ever before "except when a child, upon the loss of my own beloved mother, and ever revered and most dear grandmother!" The prospect of marriage threatens another terrible loss: that of her father and her established dependencies. Unable to face it, she opposes her father's professed wishes, retains her single state, and immediately (twenty-three years old now) begins thinking that no one will ever love her.

In this conflict as in the other internal struggles recorded in the diary of the pre-*Evelina* years, one feels an adolescent uncertainty of identity but little uncertainty of action. Miss Burney possesses already a strong impulse to reject: to push away impropriety and to forestall impingement. The force of public opinion has for her the status of a concrete reality with high potential for personal damage. By avoiding impropriety, she can avoid notice and consequently threat. She wants also to preserve the securities of her protected role as daughter. The issues of her life are already defined. How can a woman evade attention, yet assert her self? How can she protect that self? How can she avoid wrongdoing without resigning herself to total passivity? What can she say without dangerous exposure?

Writing *Evelina* in secrecy and publishing it anonymously, she allowed herself some self-exposing "saying." Her resultant sense of danger and fear dominates her journal and published letters for years after the book's publication. "All that I can say for myself is," she summarizes, "that I have always feared discovery, always sought concealment, and always known that no success should counterbalance the publishing my name." She has supported this statement in advance with abundant instances of a terror of discovery that seems, like her early guilt about writing, to bear a distinctly sexual aspect. When Mrs. Thrale accuses her of "an over-delicacy that may make you unhappy all your life," she explains that she had thought herself "as safe" with the publisher Lowndes as when her manuscript lay in her own bureau drawer. To be "known as a scribbler" threatens her impregnability. She "trembles" and worries about her possible "downfall" as a writer. "I would a thousand times rather forfeit my character as a writer," she explains, "than risk ridicule or censure as a female." At the age of sixty-two, looking back over a successful career, she remarks that "never yet had the moment arrived in which to be marked had not been embarrassing and disconcerting to me, even when most flattering."

To be marked, discovered, known as a writer, and, therefore, perhaps not a proper female, perhaps a woman unforgivably addicted to self-display: this idea focused Fanny Burney's terror of doing wrong. To make oneself known as a writer invites people to look; to offer one's fantasies for the perusal of others invites violation. For a woman to be looked at or talked of means, at best, loss of dignity, at worst, loss of reputation. Lured into discussion of "learning in woman," Miss Burney confesses her belief that "it has no recommendation of sufficient value to compensate its evil excitement of envy and satire." When her half sister, Sarah Burney, visits her after her mother's death, Fanny acknowledges her virtues and skills but complains at length about the fact that the young woman (twenty-five years old) wishes her accomplishments recognized. "She has many excellent qualities . . . but she is good enough to make me lament that she is not modest enough to be yet better."

Loss of modesty amounts to loss of virtue; only by strict decorum can a woman protect herself. From 1786 to 1791, her journal and letters make clear, Miss Burney committed herself absolutely to propriety in her service to Queen Charlotte. Her court experience, as she reports it, emphasizes the degree to which her life was assuming what seems in retrospect the symmetrical development of a carefully worked-out drama. First had come the questioning adolescence, in which social fear triumphed over daring impulse without ever quite extinguishing it; then followed a social pattern paralleled by that of Miss Burney's literary life, in which the writing of a second novel (to be published in secret) succeeded the destruction of the first, which she had felt to be entirely impermissible. Finally came the young adult years in which Fanny Burney struggled with the sense of exposure created by sucessful authorship. She wrote a comedy but withdrew it from public view at her father's suggestion of possible impropriety. She labored over a second publishable novel of unimpeachable morality, explaining, to the point of tedium, here impeccable purposes, soliciting and accepting frequent advice from all her mentors, as if to lessen the potential burden of notoriety and the conceivable imputation of seeking it. But no amount of self-guarding or protestation could resolve her guilt at self-display. Acceptance of the court position represented an attempt to find solution at the opposite extreme. Sinking herself in a role, giving up writing for publication, governing herself entirely by external expectation, she tried by total self-subordination to eliminate all conflict.

She never fancied the court position would provide personal pleasure. In accepting it, she wished above all to please her father, although she realized that her new commitment would involve relinquishing indulgence of her vital private affections. Compliance is the theme of her time at court. She comes to love the Queen, and from the start she adores Mrs. Delany, the old lady who introduced her to the royal family and whom she continues to see in her new position. Subordinating herself to such women, she believes herself thus to escape all danger of wrongdoing. But despite her devotion and her eagerness to serve, to please her father, the Queen, and Mrs. Delany, to be good and avoid evil—despite these forces urging her toward contentment, she feels bitter and unending abhorrence of her lot. She suffers from the capricious tyranny of Mrs. Schwellenberg, her immediate superior, to whom the Queen feels so deeply attached that Fanny cannot complain to her. She suffers from deprivation of real human fellowship, from the boredom of repeated ritual, and from the intense physical strain of her position.

To her sister, Mrs. Phillips, she writes, in August 1786, confessing her misery and outlining her proposed solution to it: "If to you alone I show myself in these dark colours, can you blame the plan that I have intentionally been forming—namely, to wean myself from myself—to lessen all my affections—to curb all my wishes—to deaden all my sensations?" To wean, to lessen, to curb, to deaden: a program of deprivation and reduction. A few months later, in her journal, she puts it in more positive terms.

> Now, therefore, I took shame to myself, and *Resolved to be happy*. And my success has shown me how far less chimeri-cal than it appears is such a resolution.
> To be patient under . . . disappointments . . . to relin-quish, without repining, frequent intercourse with those I love;—to settle myself in my monastery, without one idea of ever quitting it;—to study for the approbation of my lady abbess, and make it a principal source of content, as well as spring of action;—and to associate more cheerily with my surrounding nuns and monks;— these were the articles which were to support my resolution.

Despite the talk of happiness, patience, and cheeriness, she still advo-cates for herself suppression, submission, and resignation. She knows her absolute dependence on those around her. Struggling to convert it into a fact of positive meaning, she demands of herself something almost equivalent to religious conversion—her metaphor of the mon-astery suggesting her recognition of exactly this point.

The terms of the conflict between the need for self-assertion and the desire for self-concealment through conformity become more viv-idly defined during the record of the court years. The conflict itself, in fact, was probably more intense than at any other time of Fanny Burney's life because now her solution could not readily resolve the internal oppositions. Before and after her service to the Queen, Miss Burney used her fears and proprieties as means of guarding her inner life, her writing life. At Court, on the other hand, she did not write to any purpose, although she began several tragedies in an evident effort to express and contain her inner turmoil. As the imbalance increased between the demands of the world and the needs of the self, the solution was in danger of becoming the problem. Previously the young writer had met both demands simultaneously, strategies of self-concealment providing means of self-assertion. Now the strategy no longer worked. Because the journal has already established its clear vision of the personal possibilites implicit in the life of subordination, it can also sharply convey the experience of something going wrong, possibilities closing off. But it conveys, further, the consequent growth of new certainties.

During these years at Court, with their vivid experience of suppression, Fanny Burney appears to have reflected on the essential experience of women. Her own life—like the lives of her fictional heroines—confronted her with severely limited alternatives. What could she do if she left the Queen's service? She could only live with her father, doomed to be his burden unless another man took her off his hands. She could, of course, once more write for publication, but the idea of achieving independence through writing did not yet appear to occur to her. What did occur to her, although perhaps not quite consciously, was that other women in different ways duplicated her fate. She sees around her painful results of arranged marriages and subordinated female lives. In her conversations with "Mr. Turbulent," we learn of her attitudes about women. The Reverend de Guiffardière figures largely in Miss Burney's account of her court years. Apparently happily married, he nevertheless indulges in extravagant flirtation with Miss Burney, his purpose unclear. Deliberately provocative, he challenges her cherished evasions. Thus, when Miss Burney declares her unwillingness to countenance "error" in other women, Mr. Turbulent accuses her of hypocrisy. "This brought me forth. I love not to be attacked for making professions beyond my practice; and I assured him, very seriously, that I had not one voluntary acquaintance, nor one with whom I kept up the smallest intercourse of my own seeking or wilful concurrence, that had any stain in their characters that had ever reached my ears." The dialogues between Mr. Turbulent and Miss Burney dramatize the tensions of "bringing forth" such a woman. She withdraws; he pursues. She shows herself; he triumphs. What she says makes no difference to him, only whether she is willing to say anything at all. Although she prides herself on not engaging in debate, he forces her to participate. Finally she makes the fact of his forcing the source of her victory.

> "And pray, Mr. Turbulent, solve me, then, this difficulty: what choice has a poor female with whom she may converse? Must she not, in company as in dancing, take up with those who choose to take up with her?"

He was staggered by this question, and while he wavered how to answer it, I pursued my little advantage—

"No man, Mr. Turbulent, has any cause to be flattered that a woman talks with him, while it is only in reply; for though *he* may come, go, address or neglect, and do as he will,—she, let her think and wish what she may, must only follow as he leads."

In dancing, in company, in life, a woman "must only follow." Given the social demand for such subservience, compliance becomes meaningless; behind her expert cooperation, the woman thinks and wishes as she will. True, she cannot act upon her thoughts and wishes. Equally, she cannot be compelled to expose them. Mr. Turbulent is quite naturally "staggered." No matter what he drives Miss Burney to say, she can claim finally to have said it for his sake, not her own. Her thoughts and wishes remain her own—not to be "brought forth," never shown. Beginning to identify her tactics and her need for them as consequences of her sex, she gains force in her modest self-assertions, now able to claim the power of her privacy without justifying it by literary productivity. Such journal sequences as the account of the conversation with Mr. Turbulent have more profound literary merits than their authentic renditions of speech. They reveal a rich imagining of the conventionally disguised self. Miss Burney convinces the reader, just as she convinces Mr. Turbulent, that much lies beneath her compliance. Without revealing her own depths, she evokes their mysterious existence. Her life of emotional deprivation gradually gives her the survivor's strength. Unhappy, she learns to maintain herself; her diaries evoke the drama of her survival and her strengthening.

Miss Burney's elaborate fears, with the avoidances they generate, create for her in her maturity a rather distinct identity, although one which would require formulation in largely negative terms. She identifies herself as a woman in hiding, the product of a feminine discipline of fear, but this identity does not altogether satisfy her. Her youthful concern with freedom has not vanished. Although she reaps psychic benefits from her flawless conformity, she also pays large costs. Mrs. Schwellenberg insists that she keep the window down on her side of the carriage, to provide air. A sharp wind seriously inflames her eyes. Her father, seeing the consequences of obedience to such authority, orders her to insist that the glass remain raised on subsequent expeditions. "I was truly glad of this permission to rebel, and it has given me an internal hardiness in all similar assaults, that has at least relieved my mind from the terror of giving mortal offence where most I owe implicit obedience, should provocation overpower my capacity of forbearance." Permission to rebel! Yearning for freedom, Fanny Burney requires that it be given her. She pleads with her father to allow her to abandon court life, which has not only damaged her health but forced her to live "like an orphan—like one who had no natural ties, and must make her way as she could by those that were factitious." Claiming her entitlement to parental nurturance, her right to a woman's life of feelings, she returns to the original safety of her father's house.

This choice, however, seems not to have been so regressive as it may appear. In some ways it indeed involves a return to the status and the feelings of adolescence. Fanny begins writing again—"merely scribbling what will not be repressed"—thus providing "a delight to my dear Father inexpressibly great." He hardly cares what she writes; neither, apparently, does she. She makes no attempt to publish anything, still fully convinced of the danger of exposure. At the age of forty she writes, "the panics I have felt upon entering to any strange company, or large party even of intimates, has [sic], at times, been a suffering unspeakably, almost incredibly severe to me." Fear continues to provide the principle not only of her conduct but of her very being.

Such a woman, it seems evident, could hardly hope to marry, to make a positive commitment that would separate her from her beloved father. Yet marry she did, uniting herself with a man of different culture and religion, a man capable of providing no economic security, and most startling of all, one whom her father thought an inappropriate match. Her father did not attend her wedding. The psychic process that made it possible involved the rationalization of old patterns into new forms. As feeling urged her in unfamiliar directions, she discovered how the fear of wrongdoing could justify satisfying her desires. M. D'Arblay's position as persecuted victim of political injustice made it seem wrong to cause him further unhappiness by refusing to gratify him. Moreover, the Frenchman, it turned out, could assume a position in Miss Burney's life morally comparable to that of Mrs. Delany and Queen Charlotte. If they had functioned for her as substitute grandmother and mother (she suggests these terms herself), M. D'Arblay could take the moral stance of father—that posture characteristic of all Fanny Burney's novelistic heroes, beginning with Evelina's Lord Orville. In early April 1793, Fanny writes to her sister: "His nobleness of character—his sweetness of disposition—his Honour, Truth, integrity—

with so much of softness, delicacy, & tender humanity—except my beloved Father & Mr. Lock, I have never seen such a man in this world, though I have drawn such in my Imagination." The man of her dreams, in short, must be a moral paragon. She has no doubt of her suitor's power to make her happy; she only questions her own reciprocal capacity. The next month, he rebukes her for failing to write her sister frequently enough. "I own I had an odd feel at the sort of authority that might seem implied in the reproof. But this noble Creature will spare no one & no thing that he holds wrong. I vindicated myself . . . He heard my justification with a look of serious attention that made me internally smile & *look forward*—for it said, 'I MUST ALWAYS FULLY understand that you do RIGHT.—' 'Tis well I have no intention to do otherwise!—Oh my Susan! if it should, indeed, be my lot to fall into the hands of one so scrupulous in integrity, how thankfully shall I hail my Fate!" Her rhapsodic tone, inspired by his rigorous demands on her, sounds perfectly genuine, as does her formulation of marriage as a commitment requiring only passive acceptance. Because M. D'Arblay assumes the position of moral mentor, she can avoid wrongdoing by marrying him, for she is both helping a needy man (her pension from the Queen supported them both) and submitting to the guidance of one whom she considers her moral superior. Her union with him marks the climax of her story. Reporting it, she emphasizes the degree to which it confirms her identity, while enlarging her sense of possibility.

"Can you conceive any thing equal to my surprise," one of her sisters wrote to another, "at hearing our vestal sister had ventured on that stormy sea of matrimony." Fanny explains that she married in search of happiness, which for her must derive from "Domestic comfort & social affection." Moreover, "M. d'Arblay has a taste for literature, & a passion for reading & writing as marked as my own; this is a simpathy to rob retirement of all superfluous leisure, & ensure to us both occupation constantly edifying or entertaining. He has seen so much of life, & has suffered so severely from its disappointments, that retreat, with a chosen Companion, is become his final desire." Thus she fantasizes an ideal situation (an ideal, incidentally, which she very nearly achieved): retreat from the world and final commitment to the life of avoidance with a husband unable to find employment in England; a life of the affections as well, that existence of feeling and emotional security for which she had yearned; pseudoparental permission to indulge her passion for reading and writing at the side of a man who shared and condoned it.

Mme. D'Arblay knows the general astonishment at her marriage and professes that her own amazement exceeds that of "all my Friends united." From the new safety of matrimony she asserts a distinct and positive sense of self. Despite, or perhaps because of, her long training and eager participation in the rituals of female compliance, she has developed a "specialness" of character and taste that any conceivable husband must conform to rather than hope to change. Only with such a man would the hazard of marriage diminish, its promise expand, and the likelihood of happiness seem greater than that in a state of such autonomy as a single woman could hope to achieve. In fact autonomy, for Fanny Burney, felt less desirable than sympathy. Liberty of feeling and expression would be infinitely less dangerous if someone shared her feelings and approved her expression. Long accustomed to following external dictates, she could best discover her own will through another. Thus, writing to Mrs. Waddington about her pregnancy, she reveals her physical terror of childbirth and comments, "My Partner, however, who daily encreases the debt I owe him of my life's happiness, rejoices—& I must be a wretch of ingratitude & insensibility to regret whatever he can wish." Still formulating her responsibilities in terms of what she must *not* do, she attributes the wish for parenthood to her husband alone and gains moral strength for her ordeal by interpreting it as something done for the sake of another.

Through the "Social Simpathy" she found with D'Arblay, the writer once more could write for the public, her sense of the potential indecency of such display counteracted by her conviction that her writing, too, served the interests of others, helping to support her husband and son. "I had previously determined," she observes, "when I *changed my state*, to set aside all my innate & original abhorrences, & regard & use as resources MYSELF, what had always been considered as such by others." Others had long valued the products of her fantasy. Now she could value them herself, as the source of economic security, and she expresses openly her desire to drive the best possible bargain for her work. No longer wrongdoing to be avoided and less vividly an inlet for danger, the writing of novels had become virtuous. It provided a way of articulating her own good principles and of exorcising her dangerous impulses, and provided also means of supporting her family.

The mature identity asserted in the journals depends on a rich acceptance of roles. Mme. D'Arblay conveys herself as wife, mother, and writer. The three roles comfortably interchange and merge, the first two creating a screen for the third. Secure in her understanding of her writing as means to a noble end, she need worry no longer about why she feels compelled to write. Her fears of the world are held at bay by the solidity of her domestic position. She writes charmingly and perceptively of her son's development and expresses with increasing ease and freedom her opinions about the vexed affairs of her extended family, rich in disastrous marriages, unexpected elopements, unmentionable adulteries, all of which Fanny contemplates serenely from her domestic retreat. She survives twelve years of postrevolutionary France with aplomb, occupying herself with her last novel, intended to support her son at Cambridge University. Hostile criticism seems less terrifying than it had earlier appeared. Income matters more than praise or blame.

Yet Fanny Burney never outgrew her woman's dependence on the approval of those she loved. She had been right in her premarital assessment of her husband. His sympathy with her wishes and purposes was almost total. But when, in 1800—she was forty-eight years old—her father disapproved an attempt to produce her comedy, *Love and Fashion*, she reveals the continued potency of early conflict. Withdrawing the play, she yet movingly begs her father to allow her the liberty he claims for himself. "Leap the pales of your paddock," she urges him to tell her—"let us pursue our career; and, while you frisk from novel to comedy, I, quitting Music and Prose, will try a race with Poetry and the Stars." (Dr. Burney was writing a long poem about astronomy.) Immediately, guilt ensues: "I am sure my dear father will not infer, from this appeal, I mean to parallel our work. No one more truly measures her own inferiority, which, with respect to yours, has always been my pride. I only mean to show, that if my muse loves a little variety, she has a hereditary claim to try it." The same emotional ambivalence (here manifest even in sentence structure: is she comparing her inferiority to his inferiority?) controlled much of her life: on the one hand, the longing to "leap the pales," on the other, the inability to do so without parental permission. Her tone indicates resentment of enforced inferiority although she asserts her pride in the inferiority that has constituted a woman's (or a girl's) security. The devious appeal to parental emotion, with the reference to "hereditary claim," possibly recalls to the reader if not the writer that earlier deviousness by which Miss Burney reminded her father that he had caused her to live "like an orphan" at Court. Playing on her father's guilt and revealing her own, she suggests how she has both used and been controlled by fears that originate in the child's dependent condition.

It may appear that I have been telling the story of Fanny Burney's life. In fact I have been summarizing her story of her life as it emerges through the evolving record of the letters and diaries. Only by the diarist's interpretation do we learn that the important aspect of publishing a novel is that people look at you and that her husband's moral impeccability makes her marriage possible. The story of her life, as the journals and letters tell it, dramatizes the freedoms and the restrictions of fear. Its narrative strength derives from its singleness of interpretation. The principles of self-concealment that appear to have controlled Fanny Burney's life control her telling of that life (and are reinforced by that telling), giving to her story, despite the fact that it is composed of disparate small units, integrity of purpose and coherence of form. The unmastered conflict that muddles Mrs. Pilkington's and Mrs. Charke's literary intent, the self-pity and self-importance that mar the proportions of Mrs. Thrale's story here yield to literary and moral clarity. Although such clarity implies the embracing of limitation, it is a principle of power. At least as consciously as her predecessors, Fanny Burney writes of herself specifically as a woman. Her grasp on a woman's resources, however, extends to their literary possibilities.

Virginia Woolf, reflecting on her own keeping of a diary, wrote:

> There looms ahead of me the shadow of some kind of form which a diary might attain to. I might in the course of time learn what it is that one can make of this loose, drifting material of life; finding another use for it than the use I put it to, so much more consciously and scrupulously, in fiction . . . I should like it to resemble some deep old desk, or capacious hold-all, in which one flings a mass of odds and ends without looking them through. I should like to come back, after a year or two, and find that the collection had sorted itself and refined itself and coalesced, as such deposits so mysteriously do, into a mould, transparent enough to reflect the light of our life, and yet steady, tranquil compounds with the aloofness of a work of art.

The mysterious process of "sorting" and "coalescing," the tranquillity of a work of art—these descriptions apply also to Fanny Burney's journals, a miscellaneous repository in which dynamism and unity alike derive from the implications of commitment to fear of wrongdoing as an operative principle and as the action of the writer's life and work. Of course, to understand the journals in this way involves ignoring many of their details in an effort to perceive the underlying principle of coherence. But that principle, I would argue (as Virginia Woolf presumably would too), gives to the utterances of diary and letters their fundamental literary strength.

If the collection of Fanny Burney's journals and letters creates the effect of autobiography, a coherent narrative implying an imaginative grasp of experience, her four novels also have aspects of psychic autobiography. One can readily perceive in them versions of the journals' central theme: the discipline and the liberation of a woman's fears of disapproval and of being found wanting—fear, in fact, of the other people who comprise society. But novels, with their capacity to express wish and fantasy as well as reality, allow Fanny Burney to enlarge her communication of her own nature. Her fiction illustrates complex feminine identities of indirection.

Ian Watt, noting that women wrote most novels in the eighteenth century, hints also—in terms more tactful than mine—that most of those novels were bad. In Jane Austen, he suggests, we first encounter an unmistakable example of the fact "that the feminine sensibility was in some ways better equipped to reveal the intricacies of personal relationships and was therefore at a real advantage in the realm of the novel." He does not explain why earlier female writers had proved unable to exploit this advantage. Indeed, the fact—like many facts about literary quality—is profoundly inexplicable. One can describe the aspects of Fanny Burney's novels that make them more moving and more meaningful than Jane Barker's, and it is possible to demonstrate how Jane Austen excels Fanny Burney. *Why* is another matter; *why* reduces one to vaguenesses like *talent* and *genius*.

To define the strengths and weaknesses of Fanny Burney's fictional achievement, however, may lead at least to speculation about the reasons for her superiority to her female contemporaries. Her strengths are more far-reaching than has been generally recognized. *Evelina* has been praised as though it consisted only of a collection of skillful character sketches. Joyce Hemlow has demonstrated its affinities to the "courtesy book," as an effort to outline a scheme of acceptable womanly conduct. It has been admired ever since its own time for the accuracy of its social detail and conversation. But it also manifests a high level of psychological insight closely related to the self-knowledge that emerges from even the youthful diaries. Fanny Burney may write better fiction than other women of her era partly because she has come to terms more fully than they with the realities of the female condition. She is therefore "equipped to reveal the intricacies of personal relationships" as they actually exist in the world and is not blinded by wishful fantasy or by anger, although both manifest themselves in her work.

Self-discovery of a woman in hiding constitutes the subject of the novels, as of the journals. Fanny Burney's heroines hide specifically because they are women, driven to concealments in order to maintain their goodness. They do not, except in brief moments, openly resent their fates. Yet the tension suggested by a formulation that asserts the simultaneity of discovery and hiding pervades Miss Burney's fiction. She constructs elaborate happenings to articulate conflict, locate happiness, and apportion blame. Her transformations of life in fiction, while insisting on the essential order of experience, also hint their author's awareness of the psychic costs of such affirmation. Anxiety dominates the Burney novels, despite their happy endings. However minute its pretexts—and often they seem trivial indeed—its weight is real, deeply experienced by the central characters and, to a surprising extent, shared even by readers who can readily dismiss its nominal causes. In fact, the causes lie deep; the heroines suffer profound conflicts.

Evelina, of the four heroines, has the fewest and most trivial real problems. Like Cecilia and Juliet in *The Wanderer* she is in effect an orphan (her father, though alive, has refused to acknowledge her), but she has a benevolent guardian and devoted friends. A summary of the novel's plot will suggest, though, how profoundly it involves itself with fundamental questions of identity. Evelina is the unacknowledged daughter of an English baronet secretly married to a young woman, half French, who died in childbirth, leaving her infant to the guardianship of a benevolent clergyman until the child's father is willing to admit his marriage as well as his paternity. At the narrative's opening, Evelina, after seventeen years of rural seclusion, goes to visit a friend who soon takes her to London. There she encounters, by chance, her vulgar and disagreeable French grandmother, Mme. Duval, who insists that she associate with equally vulgar English relatives. Evelina, however, feels drawn to the aristocracy. She is sexually attracted to Lord Orville, extravagantly courted by Sir Clement Willoughby. Much of the action concerns her efforts to identify herself with the upper class—her manners are already upper class manners—and to evade her kinship with the bourgeoisie. Finally she claims acknowledgment by her true father, only to face absolute rejection as an impostor, since he believes another young woman to be his daughter. A nurse's confession reveals an earlier baby-switching trick, and the novel ends with Evelina in happy possession of, in effect, three fathers: her paternalistic new husband, Lord Orville; her virtuous guardian, Mr. Villars; and her genuine father, Sir John Belmont. All three confirm her identity of true aristocracy and virtue.

The difficulties the novel nominally concerns itself with, according to its writer's direct assertion, derive mainly from Evelina's social inexperience. Nothing happens except "little incidents," but virtue, feeling, and understanding finally receive their just reward, the heroine's "conspicuous beauty" providing the means to this appropriate end. More obviously than stories such as Jane Barker's tale of a merman and his paramour, this tale represents a familiar female fantasy: a potent vision of virtue recognized and rewarded despite its incidental errors—specifically, in this instance, Fanny Burney's own kind of virtue. But the novel has a level of realism lacking in many other fictions by female writers. It concerns itself with a young woman's entrance into a genuinely imagined social world, dominated, like Fanny Burney's own, by forms and manners, and very real in its pressures, cruelties, and arbitrary benignities. "The right line of conduct," Evelina's guardian, Mr. Villars, tells her, "is the same for both sexes:" But Mr. Villars lives quite out of the world. Right though he is in theory, and confirmed in his rightness by the wish fulfillment of the ending, he does not understand the practical problems of a woman's following the right line of conduct. Evelina has to come to terms with the disparity between his ideals (which are also hers) and the way life actually takes place in the world, but she also must avoid relinquishing, or even modifying, the standards that attest her virtue. Like Tom Jones, she must learn prudence. But prudence for her, as for Fanny Burney, constitutes mainly avoidance, and she too is perpetually, and increasingly, dominated by fear of wrongdoing.

Direct comments in the novel about the world emphasize its danger, its superficiality and hypocrisy, and its sinister power. The world threatens individual identity. Mr. Villars, living in retirement, fears its effects on Evelina. He also recognizes the world's inescapable power. Only the frivolous wholeheartedly accept worldly values, but no one escapes them. The choices for women consist mainly of options to refuse or to accept rather than possibilities to act. Evelina acts meaningfully and independently once, when—in an improbable and overwritten scene—she snatches the pistols from a suicidal young man. She then faints. "In a moment, strength and courage seemed lent me as by inspiration: I started, and rushing precipitately into the room, just caught his arm, and then, overcome by my own fears, I fell down at his side, breathless and senseless." Even when the woman possesses and displays strength and courage, she understands (or explains) them as given to her from outside, and her own powerful fears counteract her impulse toward action, reducing her to the passivity more characteristic of the female state and more unarguably blameless. Women aspire to the negative condition of blamelessness. Evelina is constantly beset by fears of being thought bold, or rude, or unwomanly. She fears acting. She writes to Mr. Villars, "Unable as I am to act for myself, or to judge what conduct I ought to pursue, how grateful do I feel myself, that I have such a guide and director to counsel and instruct me as yourself!" And, much later, she appeals in similar terms to her lover, Lord Orville. The proper line of conduct is *not* the same for both sexes. Men guide and instruct; women are guided and instructed. Evelina makes quite explicit her desire (which she shares with her creator) to find a lover or husband to fill the same role as father or guardian. She assumes the utter propriety of remaining as much as possible a child: ignorant, innocent, fearful, and irresponsible.

Proving her sagacity, her lover values her for precisely these qualities. Like Evelina's guardian, whom in many respects he resembles, he believes the world is opposed to rationality and values the woman who knows nothing of it. Shortly before he proposes, he summarizes Evelina's character for a group of his fashionable friends, explaining the occasional "strange" elements in her behavior as effects "of inexperience, timidity, and a retiring education," praising her as "informed, sensible, and intelligent," and glorifying "her modest worth, and fearful excellence." Fearfulness has become an index of goodness. Lord Orville recognizes the positive qualities of Evelina's mind, but he praises more the elements of her personality that encourage her to hold back from experience. Strikingly often in all Fanny Burney's novels, the terms of praise applied to women—*artless, blameless*—emphasize the negative: the refrainings induced by fear.

But *Evelina* also contains one minor woman character who does not refrain: the redoubtable Mrs. Selwyn. "She is extremely clever; her understanding, indeed, may be called *masculine;* but, unfortunately, her manners deserve the same epithet; for, in studying to acquire the knowl-

edge of the other sex, she has lost all the softness of her own." No one
likes Mrs. Selwyn, and since a woman's fate in the world depends
largely on the degree to which she is liked, this fact alone presumably
urges negative judgment of a female who feels entitled on the basis of
her strong mind to act aggressively in company. She alone, for
instance, feels free to remark devastatingly (and accurately) on masculine idiocy in the presence of its perpetrators. Evelina observes that this
habit makes enemies; she does not comment on the accuracy of Mrs.
Selwyn's judgment. Fanny Burney, disclaiming responsibility for
Mrs. Selwyn through her heroine's disapproval, yet allows her to
remain a provocative image of female intelligence and force. The
novelist thus suggests that she is aware, although she has not yet fully
acknowledged it, that Evelina's choices, proper as they are, do not
exhaust the tempting possibilities for intelligent women.

Evelina chooses dependency and fear, a choice no less significant
for being thrust upon her. It amounts to the declaration of the identity
that achieves her social and economic security. The identity she cares
about most is given her from without by husband and father. The
problem in achieving her woman's identity differs from its male equivalent, from Tom Jones's search for his identity, for example. Her
education in society teaches her not to relinquish but to use her
innocence and her fears. The discovery of prudence enables her to
form new dependency relations. No better solution for women is fully
realized in the novel. Yet that disturbing figure, Mrs. Selwyn, who
expresses female hostilty toward the male without suffering any pen-
alty beyond general dislike, whose mind and money make her sufficiently powerful to resist or endure dislike, suggests an alternative to
the dominant fantasy of the woman rewarded for innocence by the
dream of scorning the world's judgment while forcing its notice.

But the dominant dream of female withdrawal that preserves
individual integrity, protects private feeling, and attracts the perfect
lover suggests more clearly than any utterance in her diary the young
author's longings and hopes. *Evelina*, like the letters and journals,
concentrates on a woman's attempt to preserve and defend herself with
the few obvious resources at her disposal. The success of that attempt
reaffirms Fanny Burney's personal decisions.

Novels—at least eighteenth-century novels—differ from autobiog-
raphies and journals partly in their detailed attention to characters other
than the protagonist. Women novelists on the whole had trouble
dealing with this aspect of their craft; rarely did they succeed in

evoking more than the single female character at the center of their narratives. (In some instances, of course, not even the heroine, paragon rather than recognizable person, was convincingly evoked.) Fanny Burney, on the other hand, seemed to find multiple characterization a vital expressive resource. Through the people she makes Evelina encounter she manages to convey considerable, and rather complicated, hostility. Lord Orville and Mr. Villars, both exemplary males, actually engage little of her attention: they remain wooden presences. But the large cast of distasteful aristocrats, the equally unattractive petty bourgeoisie, sadistic Captain Mirvan, and vulgar but vigorous Mme. Duval—these figures come splendidly to life. Their satiric portrayal enables the writer to express and to justify her vivid antagonisms. Mrs. Selwyn provides a direct mouthpiece for aggressive impulses, but Miss Burney also conveys aggression through her derogatory character sketches and through her repeated invention of actions expressing extreme hostility: Captain Mirvan's plot to make Mme. Duval think herself beset by highwaymen, the race of two ancient women arranged by the aristocrats, the scene in which Sir Clement is bitten by a monkey.

As autobiography, in other words, this novel reveals more than the diaries. Allowing Miss Burney to articulate repressed aspects of her personality, it reminds us of the degree to which her constant professions of fear and her insistent withdrawals represent not true timidity but a socially acceptable device of self-protection. The writing and publishing of novels—a public act—also involves self-protection; no one holds the author personally responsible for Captain Mirvan's sadism or Mrs. Selwyn's ferocious commentary. Through imagining such sadism and such commentary, she permits herself the impermissible. She both declares the high value of her own mode of dealing with the world and compensates for the restrictions of her propriety.

No one now reads Fanny Burney's novels, except for *Evelina*, where comedy and youthful exuberance qualify the pervasive anxiety and one can even smile at the anxiety, for its causes are, by and large, so trivial. Yet the later novels, creaky of plot and increasingly impenetrable in rhetoric, seriously explore the possibilities for women to assert individual identities. More clearly than Fanny Burney's letters and diaries, the novels betray her anger at the female condition, although she also acknowledges the possibility of happiness within that condition. Imagining female defiance, she imagines also its futility in those heroines dominated, like herself, by fears of doing wrong. The atmosphere of anxiety she vividly evokes suggests what conflicts attend a woman's search for identity. The Burney female characters face endless struggle between what they want to have (independence, specific husbands, friends, pleasure, work) and what they want to be (angelically perfect): between the impulses to action and to avoidance. However important or negligible the specific images of this conflict, it stands behind the action and the characterization of all the novels.

The record of the journals, extending chronologically far beyond the writer's marriage, makes it clear that her commitment to D'Arblay, fulfilling as it was, did not mark the happy ending to her experience as it did for all her fictional heroines. Marriage resolved or simplified conflicts, granting Fanny Burney permission to act (through writing) while yet remaining conspicuously good; it thus provided energy. It also generated new dramas: classic Oedipal struggles, symbolic dilemmas about where and how to live, and conflicts of interest between Fanny's old family and her new—dramas that the journals expose more freely than they had revealed the problems of the author's youth, although in fact the problems remain in many respects essentially the same. The plot of the diaries thus necessarily differs from that of the novels, which never explore postmarital experience.

Yet the fictional inventions uncover the inner realities of the writer's mature as well as her youthful life. Indeed, comparison of Fanny Burney's personal record with her novels suggests the possibility that fiction may more vividly than autobiography delineate the shape of an author's private drama. The external events of Miss Burney's life, as reported in her diaries, supply small excitements, minor clashes, and tiny resolutions. The events of her novels increasingly emphasize important happenings—in *The Wanderer*, political as well as personal happening. Her heroines must cope with grotesque misunderstandings, malicious enemies, and bitter strokes of fate. They suffer more than they can comprehend—more perhaps even than their author comprehends. They express both their creator's wishes and her conviction that such wishes must be punished: the real essence of the inner drama that is more palely reflected in the relatively trivial events she chooses to record in diary and letters.

Fiction is fantasy. Both the strength and the weakness of Fanny Burney's novels derives from this fact. The books betray their author's longing for more grandiose experience than her powerful sense of decorum would allow her even to know she wanted. All except *Cecilia*, that fable of the poor little rich girl, rely on the deeply satisfying fairy-tale structure in which the hero (in these cases the heroine) with no apparent assets survives a series of demanding tests, winning by the power of goodness, triumphing over those seemingly more advantaged, and finally achieving the royal marriage that symbolizes lasting good fortune. But Fanny Burney betrays conflicting fantasies, which lessen her fiction's energy: on the one hand the dream of self-assertion and success in the face of all obstacles, on the other the fearful fantasy of nemesis for female admission of hostility and female attempts at self-determination. However she heightens happenings to melodramatic impossibility, ignoring logic and straining rhetoric to insist on the importance of her tale, her stories work against themselves. In her direct accounts of herself, with her sense of morality firmly in control, the conflict between the impulse to freedom and the commitment to propriety—its resolution in action always predictable and its emotional dynamics often compelling— shapes a persuasive narrative. But the world of fiction holds forth the possibilities of greater freedom, possibilities that Fanny Burney could not adequately handle, although they enabled her to reveal herself.

Fiction is form, and form is fiction. The forms that tempted Miss Burney, in life and in literature, were moral structures that assured her that virtue found its reward. Around her she could see evidence to the contrary, particularly in female fates. Her stepsister Maria and her beloved sister Susanna both married brutes and suffered dire consequences. Susanna died after some years of Irish exile necessitated by her husband's arbitrary decisions. Marriage in real life constituted punishment as often as reward. The structures of fiction, as structures of moral order, made sense of experience. They could be imposed also on records of life. Fanny Burney's narrative of herself, in diary and letters, interpreting all conflict as moral conflict and every choice as an effort to determine the good, rationalizes her relatively quiet life as a struggle for virtue and her happy marriage as virtue's reward. It thus creates shape out of a life's random sequence of events—but a shape, significantly, of conflict.

Fiction is public communication. Fanny Burney's consciousness of this fact expresses itself, characteristically, most often in statements of what she has left out of her novels in order to avoid contaminating young minds. Thus, she boasts that *Camilla* contains no politics because "they were not a *feminine* subject for discussion" and "it would be a better office to general Readers to carry them wide of all politics, to their domestic fire sides." As usual, she is avoiding wrong. But public communication has a positive as well as a negative aspect. In the youthful diaries, writing for "nobody," Fanny expressed a deprecating sense of self; all her letters and diaries insist upon her modesty. The more impersonal expression of fiction enabled her to enlarge her self-image by splitting herself into infinitely virtuous heroines and ingeniously aggressive minor characters, by dramatizing her sense of virtue through those heroines who suffer endlessly in their efforts toward the right, and by expressing ideas that she could not allow herself to endorse through such figures as Mrs. Selwyn and Elinor Joddrell. Only in rare moments of the private record—as when she complains that Mrs. Thrale showers her with too many gifts—does Fanny Burney betray her hostility. The open record of fiction provided greater protection: she could simultaneously convey both anger and her disapproval of anger. Much more successfully than her female contemporaries, she found ways to manipulate and use her own psychic experience, not simply to avoid it through wishful fantasy or ethical didacticism.

Fiction, finally, may constitute autobiography. Through Fanny Burney's novels, through their flaws and their positive achievements, she conveys her private self more emphatically, more explicitly, than she does in the diaries. Not needing to exercise reductive moral control over every character, she can use her fantasies to communicate her feelings and her conflicts, the interior drama that her decorous life largely concealed. She quotes Mme. de Genlis: "The life of every Woman is a Romance!" The remark, implying an interpretation of actual experience in terms of literary categories, suggests a useful way to read the diaries and letters—perceiving the extent to which, even in her personal record, it is Fanny Burney's fictions that reveal herself. Writing novels, she allows herself to convey the impermissible sides of her nature and to enlarge the permissible. Writing journals, she confines herself largely to the surfaces of her life; yet she uncovers the depths by the unchanging form of her self-interpretation, by her wistful, persistent fantasy of flawless virtue, and by her insistence on shaping her account of all that happens to her in terms of the struggle for virtue. She tells the story of an uneventful life as a romance rich in drama.

Fanny Burney's novels and her journals alike reveal the dynamics of fear in a woman's experience. They also reveal some ways in which the imagination deals with emotion, demonstrating how useful are the disguises of fiction in clarifying the truths of personality and how much the forms and perceptions of fiction become necessary material for the autobiographer.

Evelina: A Chronicle of Assault

Judith Lowder Newton

To read this history of a young lady's entrance into the world is to read a chronicle of assault: for having made her debut in "public company," amid a round of London's most "fashionable Spring Diversions," Burney's genteel young heroine finds that she can go but few places indeed without being forced, intruded upon, seized, kidnapped, or in some other way violated by a male. At her first assembly she is provoked by the "negligent impertinence" of a fop, at her second "tormented . . . to death" by a baronet. A trip to the opera marks her first kidnapping, an evening at the play a public attack. At the Pantheon a lord affronts her by staring; at Vauxhall "gentlemen" "rudely" seize upon and pursue her; and at Marylebone, when she loses her party and her way, she finds that her distress "only furnished a pretence for impertinent witticisms" on the part of "bold and unfeeling" males. Burney's *Evelina*, in fact, presents us with a world dominated by the imposition of men upon women, a world in which male control takes the form of assault, and a world in which male assault is the most central expression of power.

That the author of *Evelina*, herself a young woman of good family, should give this emphasis to male control, that she should portray male control as violation, and that she should virtually equate a young lady's entry into the world with her subjection to abuse expresses something pointed about the situation of genteel unmarried women in 1778. It evokes the fact that the status of young middle-class

From *Women, Power and Subversion: Social Strategies in British Fiction, 1778–1860.* © 1981 by the University of Georgia Press.

women was in doubt; it suggests that men felt a special authority to impose their will upon them; and it implies that respectable unmarried women were essentially powerless to avoid if not to resist this imposition. *Evelina*, in fact, evokes Burney's own experience of this general historical situation, for in 1775, only one year before she wrote the major part of her novel, Fanny Burney suffered what might be termed a species of male assault upon her status and autonomy.

Burney was then twenty-three, self-educated, evidently destined for marriage, interested in love but harboring some distaste for the awkward rituals of courtship, and liable to feel, with a distinct sense of her own autonomy, that "upon the whole, the most dignified thing for an exalted female must be to die an old maid." She enjoyed, too, unusual freedom in disposing of her own time, "following my own vagaries which my papa never controls," and she had besides a sense of personal status and value. She served as amanuensis to the great Dr. Burney, and she was engaged in writing long and witty journal letters to an admiring Mr. Crisp: "Send me a minute Journal of every thing, and never mind their being trifles—trifles well-dressed, are excellent food, and your cookery is (with me) of established reputation."

The Burney family, moreover, though it had humble connections, was at least uneasily genteel. If Dr. Burney was a mere music teacher, he was also a respected scholar with an Oxford degree, and though his family remained to some extent "such sort of people," he himself entered easily into the great world. His was not a family either to worry about finance for, though money for dowries was not to be had, there were funds to send one of Fanny's brothers to Cambridge and two of her sisters to France, and Burney's diary is free of those allusions to economy which so dominate the letters of Jane Austen. It came, then, as a shock that, at twenty-three, Fanny should be pressured to place herself upon the market, should be urged to consider marrying a man she hardly knew and did not care for—and this chiefly for his money.

It was in May of 1775, shortly before her twenty-fourth birthday, that Fanny received a declaration of sorts from a Mr. Barlow, an unremarkable young man whom she had met at tea four days before and whom—it is hardly surprising—she was eager to refuse: "I am too spoilt," she wrote, "by such men as my father and Mr. Crisp to content myself with a character merely inoffensive. I should expire of fatigue with him." But Dr. Burney had several daughters without dowries, and Fanny, to her dismay, was urged by her sister, her grandmother, her maiden aunts, and her dear friend Daddy Crisp to consider the economics of her situation—Mr. Barlow too appeared provokingly "sanguine" at first about her acceptance. Mr. Crisp, for example, after recommending what he had heard of Mr. Barlow's disposition, went on to "the grand object of enquiry," Mr. Barlow's fortune:

> Is he of any profession, or only of an independent fortune? is either, or both, sufficient to promise . . . a comfortable [income]? You may live to the age of your grandmother, and not meet with so valuable an offer. . . . Look round you, Fan; look at your aunts; *Fanny Burney* won't always be what she is now! Mrs. Hamilton once had an offer of £3,000-a-year, or near it; a parcel of young giggling girls laugh'd her out of it. The man, forsooth, was not quite smart enough, though otherwise estimable. Oh, Fan, this is not a marrying age, without a handsome Fortune! . . . Suppose you lose your father,—take in all chances. Consider the situation of an unprotected, unprovided woman!

The letter was well intended, but that Daddy Crisp, a model of gentility and a sort of father-monitor as well, should ask her to consider a man she did not know and could not love, and all for the sake of an establishment, obviously pained Fanny and took her by surprise: "[Mr. Crisp] has written me such a letter! God knows how I shall answer it! Every body is against me but my beloved father." And then, perhaps a week later, Dr. Burney joined the cause, spoke to her "in favour of Mr. Barlow," and urged her not to be "peremptory" in her answer. The effect was devastating: Fanny felt assailed yet powerless to resist:

> I was terrified to death. I felt the utter impossibility of resisting not merely my father's *persuasion*, but even his advice. . . . I wept like an infant, when alone; ate nothing; seemed as if already married and passed the whole day in more misery than, merely on my own account, I ever did in my life, except [when a child] upon the loss of my own beloved mother, and ever revered and most dear grandmother!

The extent of her suffering, however, moved Dr. Burney to relent, and that very evening Fanny went to bed "light, happy, and thankful, as if escaped from destruction." On May 16 she wrote Daddy Crisp, asking forgiveness but maintaining that she was unable to act "from *worldly motives*," declaring herself "QUITE FIXED," and explaining that she had "long accustomed [herself] to the idea of being an old maid"; and so, for the most part, the affair of Mr. Barlow was ended. But it could not have ended, one assumes, without leaving its trace, without putting Fanny in some doubt about the inviolability of her status and freedom. *Evelina*, which was written largely in the following year, gives all evidence of being a mode of coming to terms with this experience, the experience of being placed upon the market, the experience of being regarded with sanguinity by an unremarkable young man, the experience of being made to lose status and power—the experience, in short, of undergoing a species of assault.

What, in a general sense, lay behind this incursion upon Burney's status and autonomy was to a large degree the declining economic stature of genteel young women in the eighteenth century, for women of all stations had lost and were continuing to lose their previously recognized economic value. The working of household plots, the home production of household articles, the participation in family industry were all in decline, and the economic drift was to make women, especially women of the middle orders, more dependent economically upon men and men less recognizably dependent upon the domestic work of women. This decline in recognized economic value enforced women's traditionally subordinate position in relation to men, a phenomenon that did not go unnoticed by the age. Defoe, for one, understood that women's lower status went hand in hand with their loss of economic function, and he suggests that men took advantage of the situation: "They will not make them useful that they may not value themselves upon it, and make themselves, as it were, the equals of their husbands."

The waning status of single dependent women in particular is also suggested by a familiar shift in the use of the word "spinster." Once a positive term for female manufacturers and a reflection of the importance that unmarried women had enjoyed as participants in family industry, "spinster" became, early in the eighteenth century, a term of opprobrium for women beyond the usual age for marriage. By implication, then, dependent women of the middle orders lost status because they ceased to be or to be seen as economic assets to the family and became instead liabilities. This state of things was particularly difficult for women like Fanny Burney, women with aspirations to gentility, for they were prohibited by the definitions of gentility itself from being employed outside the home—at low wages and in occupations already glutted with women from poorer backgrounds—while inside the home fashion, at least, increasingly required them to be idle. More than one father must have advised his daughters, as did Dr. Gregory, to take up needlework that they might have something to occupy their time, for Thomas Gisborne notes that young women in general were unsuccessful in their efforts to "quicken and enliven the slow-paced hours."

All a respectable young woman could really do to ease the strain of her dependency, and the uneasy status which such dependency entailed, was to marry. But the possibility of marriage in the late eighteenth century, as Daddy Crisp suggests, was becoming increasingly unlikely. Men were marrying late, perhaps because wives were now luxury items, and when men did marry they were liable to require a dowry. Gisborne, in fact, reflects a late eighteenth-century conviction when he suggests that marriage among the middle and upper middle classes was openly becoming a mercantile matter—where a "calculating broker" pored over pedigrees, summed up the property in hand, and computed "at the market price" what a young woman was worth. On top of this, the number of women appears to have exceeded the number of men, all of which must have endorsed the traditionally superior status of single men while it enforced a general lowering of status for single women. For, once young women were of an age for marriage, they were still vulnerable to being seen as liabilities and now as liabilities in overplentiful supply. If, within the family, many single women felt like burdens, the unfavorable conditions of the marriage market must have imposed upon them the even lower identity of merchandise, and it is precisely the discomfort, the oppression of being rendered merchandise, which Burney encounters in *Evelina,* and which she reinvokes as the experience of being assaulted by men.

II

Evelina finds Burney firmly committed to the ideology that marriage is a woman's natural and only destiny and to the understanding that she achieves that destiny by displaying herself and waiting to be chosen. Given Burney's own trauma on the marriage market, this is a commitment which suggests how impoverished any other options must have appeared. Evelina's entrance into the world, like Fanny

Burney's, is patently an entry onto the marriage market, and the assemblies, operas, plays, and pleasure gardens, while initiating her into knowledge of society, also function as occasions upon which she is displayed. Indeed, there is some fun early in the novel when Evelina describes the sensation of turning herself out London-style: "You can't think how oddly my head feels; full of powder and black pins, and a great cushion on the top of it." Being an object is odd, but it is also amusing, and it is even thrilling when the princely Lord Orville asks one to dance. But being on display, which is necessary to secure a husband, to fulfill one's destiny, and to be supported, is pleasant only when one is regarded as a fascinating treasure. Unfortunately, the logic of women's economic situation dictates that she may also be regarded as something of lower value—as overstocked merchandise, for example, by men of the lower orders or, at best, by gentlemen as prey.

The workings of this logic are widely, though intuitively, evoked in *Evelina*, for it is women's economic dependency which lurks behind men's easy assumption that Evelina may be pursued, imposed upon, and controlled. Burney, moreover, although she never protests or makes a point of the fact that it *is* a woman's destiny to display herself on the market, is one of the few writers in the century to describe the experience in such a way as to emphasize its discomfort and oppression—and she is one of the very few to take this discomfort seriously. The language of Evelina's response to male assault—she is "provoked," "distressed," "terrified," "angered"—impresses upon us what ought to be obvious—that Evelina finds it oppressive to be raped—and that critics have not noticed this aspect of the novel is merely a comment on what we have come to accept as women's due.

But, while intuitively evoking the discomfort of being forcibly reduced to merchandise or prey, Burney maintains another ideological version of a genteel woman's situation and of her relation to society, a version which is much in conflict with the first. This second version suggests not only that genteel women are not merchandise at all but that there are no shared economic conditions which would tend to impose that identity upon them. And it is this vision of a genteel woman's lot that ameliorates the inescapable experience of being assailed and that ultimately helps establish an eighteenth-century patriarchy, with all its restrictions on young women, as something bearable by and indeed beneficial to young women of the middle classes.

In establishing this vision, Burney simply omits from the novel the economic conditions which in her own life and in the lives of women like her most restricted autonomy and lowered status and which also enforced the authority which men of the middle and landed orders felt in relation to women. Evelina, for example, is a woman of independent fortune, a fact which sets her quite apart from Fanny Burney and probably from the majority of women of good family. Evelina's fortune will not sustain her in a life of fashion, but it may "make her happy, if she is disposed to be so in private life"; and, while hopes of a good marriage are entertained for her by Mr. Villars (her guardian, a character based to some extent on Daddy Crisp), Evelina will never be required to consider a stiff and unremarkable young man for the sake, say, of £3,000 a year. But it is not only Evelina who escapes economic restriction. The general economic inequities of men's and women's lives are also omitted from the novel. With the exception of the £30,000 which Evelina's father bestows upon her at the end of the book, we never know, as we do in Austen, how much men and women inherit; we never know how much anyone is worth. And since everyone in the novel appears at leisure, even women and men of the trading classes, we are never in contact with any inequality in access to work.

Indeed, most concern for or consciousness of money is confined to the lower orders, where it is caricatured and dismissed. It is Mr. Smith, for example, a would-be gentleman and the tenant of a silver-smith's dining room, who hints most directly at the economic contra-diction of men's and women's lots and at the resulting inequities in status and in power. Despite some hapless gestures at courtliness— blunt references to Evelina's beauty and entirely false assertions that he always studies "what the ladies like"—Smith is fond of driving home some distinctly uncourtly realities. He is aware that women are eco-nomically dependent on men, and he reminds Evelina that "marriage is all in all with the ladies; but with us gentlemen it's quite another thing!" He is also aware that he is a buyer in a buyer's market, and it pleases him to call attention to the fact that the laws of supply and demand make *him* the treasure: "there are a great many other ladies that have been proposed to me . . . so you may very well be proud . . . for I assure you, there is nobody so likely to catch me at last as yourself." The status which male privilege and the conditions of the marriage market confer on Smith provides him in turn with the agreeable conclusion that it is natural, and even desirable, to women that he impose his will on them. Smith, in fact, is "thunderstruck with amazement" when Evelina refuses the assembly tickets he has tried to force upon her, and with the self-righteousness of one who feels that society has empowered *him* to do the imposing he "thought proper to desire [she] would tell him [her] reasons."

Young Branghton, Evelina's cousin and the son and heir of a silversmith, has even fewer pretensions to courtliness than Mr. Smith; he merely assumes, with some candor, that those who can confer economic benefits have a right to dictate. He is eager, therefore, to pay for Evelina's coach fares and opera tickets and to treat her at public places, for "if I pay, I think I've a right to have it my own way." Like Mr. Smith, young Branghton is highly conscious of the fact that women depend on men and marriage, and like Smith he is fond of twitting them about their inability to impose their will on men. Indeed, his entire relation with his sisters consists of tormenting them about their lack of marriageable qualities. They will never get a man because they are "ugly enough to frighten a horse" and liable to being exposed with "all their dirty things on, and all their hair about their ears."

Consciousness of money, of its relation to men's superior status and to their control over women, is made so rude and so untenable in Branghton and Smith that it may easily be mocked. But, more than that, in Branghton and Smith the very existence of this consciousness is explained away. It is not a response, not even an exaggerated response, to economic realities but merely a habit of mind apt to be cultivated by persons among the lower orders and particularly by persons in trade. Branghton, especially, is seen as reflecting an obsessive interest in money and prices, profit and advance, weights and measures, and physical qualities in general. In this context any attention to money in its relation to women, status, and power may be put down as one more vulgarity of the lower orders, may be cast with other perversities, like references to untidy hair and dirty underclothes, may be laughed off the stage. In the guise, then, of satirizing the vulgarities of station, Burney undermines an economic consciousness which was not at all confined to the trading classes and which was, in fact, generally imposed by real economic conditions on genteel young women like herself. In the process she also mystifies the reality of the economic conditions which were sustained by a landed patriarchy as a whole and especially by men of the ruling class.

What Burney also mystifies is community—community as the locus of shared and demeaning attitudes toward women. Although almost all men in the novel are unified in their readiness to see women as merchandise or prey, we do not feel the weight of their shared attitudes as we do in, say, *Pride and Prejudice*. For one thing, Evelina, unlike Elizabeth Bennet, is distinctly a tourist, not a fixed member of a community, and we feel that she will not be in contact with these demeaning attitudes long enough to be damaged by them. And, since the community itself is most often represented by a series of ever changing social gatherings, it appears atomistic rather than organic. The same individuals may be thrown repeatedly into one another's company, but we have little sense of their *living* together, of their acting in accord for good or ill. Intuitively and defensively, Burney provides Evelina with a community essentially lacking in communal power and thereby protects her from the concerted socializing forces with which she herself was familiar.

In effect, Burney siphons off what must have seemed to her most restrictive and objectionable in a patriarchal order and either omits or confines it safely to the trading classes. These are deft although not conscious maneuvers, but they leave a certian vacuum in the history of her heroine. For if it is not a woman's economic lot and if it is not demeaning communal attitudes toward women which account for the ease with which tradesmen and gentlemen impose themselves upon Evelina, what then is it? We are left with a chronicle of assorted violations and abuses which have no overt or systematic rationale in the world of this novel.

III

There are several ways in which Burney's historical situation may have prompted her to veil the causal relation between women's economic dependency and their subjection to male control. The 1770s, for example, were not characterized by the rampant awareness of money that was to come with early industrial capitalism, and this in itself may have allowed Burney a certain ease in omitting the facts of women's economic situation from her novel and in condemning economic consciousness itself by esconcing it amid the vulgarities of the lower orders. But, most important, Burney's historical situation also offered her a reconciling ideology about genteel women. By crediting and giving value to the view that women of good family are really treasure rather than merchandise, *Evelina* reflects a renewed and widespread tendency in the late eighteenth century, especially in its literature, to idealize women of the genteel classes.

In emphasizing male violation and control, moreover, *Evelina* reflects a related cultural and literary preoccupation: the interesting habit of seeing idealized women as persons being pursued by morally inferior males. "The drama of the aggressive male checked by the virtuous woman" has been variously interpreted. But in the work of female writers like Fanny Burney the drama has been seen as an expression of the fact that women really did feel controlled and imposed upon by men and as an expression of the fact that they were prompted to counter this disturbing awarenesss with an adherence to some mitigating fiction or ideology. What we also find in Burney, however, is evidence that awareness of male oppression did not necessarily go hand in hand with objection to a patriarchal order. *Evelina*, in fact, actually celebrates the rule of landed men by implying that only ruling-class men (never women themselves) have the power to give courtly fiction the potency of ideology, have the ability, in other words, to make the equation of women and treasure seem *real*.

There is some logic, moreover, to this association, for courtly ideologies about women have traditionally been connected with landed males. They are the kinds of fiction which very powerful men have been able to afford in relation to women. In the late eighteenth century, moreover, the power of the male gentry would have been great enough to give courtliness-as-ideology some general currency, and Burney, with her family connections to the great, must have been immersed in the beliefs which ruling-class males entertained about themselves and their relations to others. In *Evelina*, at least, it is Burney's association of courtly fiction, the idealization of genteel women, with men of the ruling class that finally permits her to endorse male control, a patriarchal system in general, and the rule of landed men and to make all three seem endurable to women.

In addition, of course, it would have been futile in 1778 for someone like Burney to protest against the rule of landed men or the lot of genteel women—and, more than anything else perhaps, this lack of option and this sense of almost total male ruling-class authority make Burney the last major female writer to give credit to the courtly fictions of landed men. But, even for Burney, to endorse patriarchy, to endorse the authority of ruling-class men, is to be immersed in tension and in contradiction. One contradiction, for example, is the fact that Burney endorses the authority of landed men while demonstrating that the superior authority of the male gentry is most dramatically revealed in their ability to control and oppress women with greater success than do men of the lower orders—for it is ruling-class men who have the greatest facility in insulting Evelina on the streets, entrapping her in their carriages, and laying hands upon her in public places.

The superior control of ruling-class men is seen most pointedly in the ballroom. The rules of the dance, of course, which express social order in general, confirm all men's authority as choosers. But the lowly Mr. Smith is less adroit and less forceful than Lovel or Sir Clement in making use of his authority. *His* attempts to foist himself as a partner upon Evelina are deftly foiled by Evelina herself, with the result that Smith is forced to dance with Evelina's grandmother, Madame Duval. When Smith, "being extremely chagrined," complains of Evelina's refusal, she responds with a "total disregard" which "made him soon change the subject." Lovel, in contrast—he is a fop but still a gentleman—does not take so lightly to being deprived of authority and status. When Evelina innocently refuses him and then accepts Lord Orville, Lovel becomes indignant, abuses Evelina until she is "ready to die with shame," and then persecutes her for the rest of the novel.

Still, if men of the gentry are more effective at assault than men of the lower orders, their assaults on Evelina are, for Burney at least, easier to take. For, even in behavior, men of the ruling class imply not that Evelina is merchandise but, rather, that she is sexual prey. The distinction now may seem nonexistent, but evidently for Burney it is less invidious that Evelina be identified as Eve than that she be identified as goods, and the contempt expressed for Mr. Smith is far stronger than the disapproval directed at Lord Merton, the most openly licentious of the ruling-class males. There is reason, too, for this disparity in judgment if one considers that the first identity—sexual prey—was not only more traditional but less liable to being supported by members of one's family. Evelina and Fanny know that they are chaste, that they are not easy prey, and no one close to them could think otherwise. The second identity, however—marketable goods—is one which the economic conditions of the age had already threatened to impose on Burney and one which her family seemed inclined to endorse. When confronted with two insulting versions of a genteel woman's status, Burney instinctively and naturally focuses upon the version least likely to be given credit by family or friends.

The greatest distinction, however, between the oppressive control of ruling-class men and that of lower-class men is that the former is more evenly and more consistently overlaid with courtly fiction. The behavior of the male gentry may imply that Evelina is really Eve, but their language sustains the fiction that she is Cinderella. Lord Merton, for example, feels doubly legitimized as a ruling-class male to force his attentions on Evelina. It is his "conscious quality" which prompts his "look of libertinism" toward women in general and the bold eyes, "rude questions and free compliments" which he directs at Evelina. But as a member of the gentry Lord Merton has also tuned his gallantries to the highest pitch. He may behave as if Evelina were prey, but his "fine speeches and compliments" make her think herself a "goddess" and Lord Merton "a pagan, paying [her] adoration."

The epitome of this split between sexual assault and courtly devotion is found in Sir Clement Willoughby, a character about whom both Evelina and her creator make some paradoxical judgments. When Sir Clement rescues Evelina at Vauxhall, when he rescues her from one set of tormentors so he may prey upon her himself, he reveals that Evelina is Eve to him too. Despite his past experience of her innocence, he ignores the information that she has lost her companions and assumes that her presence in the garden is a sign of her sexual availability. This is the basis upon which most ruling-class men are ready to deal with her: despite all protestations to the effect that she is Cinderella, the fascinating treasure, the beautiful but distant object, their behavior implies that she is both prey and willing prey.

What distinguishes Sir Clement from Lord Merton, however, is the persistence with which he imposes upon his control of Evelina the courtly fiction that she *is* Cinderella. At their first encounter, for example, Sir Clement's courtly language marks a farcical counterpoint to his behavior. As he pursues Evelina about the ballroom, badgering heer with questions about the dance partner whom she has invented to avoid him, imposing his presence over her protest, and ultimately forcing her to dance, he sustains a running and sometimes hilarious pose as the powerless lover of an unreachable mistress: "it cannot be that you are so cruel! Softness itself is painted in your eyes:—You could not, surely, have the barbarity so wantonly to trifle with my misery?" This is stuff and even Evelina knows it.

Once Sir Clement has fixed upon her as his sexual prey, he employs the same courtly fiction with greater earnestness to disguise his seductive intentions and to manipulate Evelina's response. Evelina, at these moments, is usually too agitated to reflect, but Evelina, at these moments, is usually too agitated to reflect, but Burney herself maintains a clear distinction between what is truth and what is story. When Sir Clement is most in control, when he is imposing himself most forcibly, he is, ludicrously enough, the most devoted lover. After the opera, for example, having kidnapped Evelina in his carriage, having directed the driver into the London night, and having so terrified her that she is prompted to leap from the chariot door, Sir Clement seizes her and assures her that "my life is at your devotion." When Evelina strains this fiction by thrusting her head from the window and calling for aid, Sir Clement simply retreats into his role and for the moment becomes convincing as the humble lover: "Sir Clement now poured forth abundant protestations of honour, and assurances of respect, entreating my pardon for having offended me, and beseeching my good opinon."

It should be evident, I think, that Sir Clement has the honor of a rapist, perhaps a rapist *manqué,* and Burney seems conscious of this when she has Mr. Villars condemn him: "Sir Clement, though he seeks occasion to give real offence, contrives to avoid all appearance of intentional evil." Evelina, too, is allowed to turn from much of his "nonsense" with "real disgust." And yet she is permitted to forgive him, usually in the same scene and always in response to his pose as courtly lover. Here is Evelina after her first kidnapping: "he flung himself on his knees, and pleaded with so much submission, that I was really obliged to forgive him, because his humiliation made me quite ashamed." And here is Evelina after her second: "indeed, I knew not how to resist the humility of his intreaties." In her more rational moments, moreover, Evelina is allowed to prefer Sir Clement to the hapless Mr. Smith, the would-be lover whose assaults upon her are far less persistent than Sir Clement's and, from one point of view at least, less reprehensible: "It is true, no man can possibly pay me greater compliments, or make more fine speeches, than Sir Clement Willoughby: yet his language, though too flowery, is always that of a gentleman; and his address and manners are so very superior . . . that, to make any comparison between him and Mr. Smith would be extremely unjust."

What has been pilloried here as snobbishness—and Evelina *is* a snob, with Burney's approval—must also be seen as a positive response to Sir Clement's courtly fictions, a response in which Burney shares. For, despite the flimsiness of fictions like these, they may still be valued and indeed have been valued throughout history. Given the all but absolute authority of ruling-class men, given economic and social conditions which one could not alter and which tended to impose the identity of merchandise or prey, given the lack of options to marriage and the marriage market, in particular, it was perhaps all one could do to sustain, intuitively and unthinkingly, the ideologies which gave support to one's sense of value. Mr. Smith offends because he both violates Evelina's will and flaunts the social and economic context which licenses him to do so. He reminds Evelina, in other words, of the real and overpowering forces at work. Fiction is sometimes preferable to truths like these, especially when it occasionally seems to be the truth, as is the case with the apologies of Sir Clement.

What Burney unconsciously reveals, then, in Evelina's ambivalence toward Sir Clement and in her own, is that the situation of a genteel unmarried woman could force her to credit and give value to ideologies about her experience which at some level she understood to be untrue. Indeed, Burney's main response to the essentially oppressive nature of Evelina's experience and her own, her main response to what she admits about male control in Sir Clement, is to create a greater and more courtly fiction yet—and that fiction, of course, is Lord Orville. This elegant and truly polite young man of noble birth and handsome fortune, who takes upon himself the rigors of uninterrupted noblesse oblige and courtliness, is meant to represent landed patriarchy not only as it should be but as Burney wishes to believe it is. The fiction of Lord Orville, who has all the vapid perfection of wish fulfillment, is that he reverses the normal relation between male privilege and male control. While almost every other man in the novel finds in his economic and social privilege a justification for imposing his will upon others, and in particular upon women, Lord Orville, the most privileged man in the novel, converts every social and economic benefit into a motive for deferring to or reaffirming the autonomy and status of others:

> Far from being indolently satisfied with his own accomplishments, as I have already observed many men here are, though without any pretensions to his merit, he is most assiduously attentive to please and to serve all who are in his company; and, though his success is invariable, he never manifests the smallest degree of consciousness.

Lord Orville's particular value as wish fulfillment is that he confers the identity of treasure upon Evelina—not just in language but in behavior too. At the first assembly, for example, when Evelina is most at loose ends, able neither to speak nor to act as she desires and behaving least like a woman of gentility and polish, Lord Orville gently encourages her to express her will and behaves in general as if she were a person of equal if not superior status: "had I been the person of the most consequence in the room, I could not have met with more attention and respect." This affirmation of her status as treasure is most thoroughly realized in Lord Orville's courtship of Evelina, for this princely young man ignores all the usual requirements of marriage by proposing to a young woman of obscure parentage and slender means, thus permanently conferring upon her the identity of Cinderella. The wish fulfillment is so perfect and so complete that Burney is moved, rather uneasily, I think, to reassure us that the hero has not been parted from his senses:

> When I expressed my amazement that he could honour with his choice a girl who seemed so infinitely, in *every* respect, beneath his alliance, he frankly owned, that he had fully intended making more minute inquiries into my family and connections, . . . but the suddenness of my intended journey, and the uncertainty of seeing me again, put him quite off his guard, and "divesting him of prudence, left him nothing but love."

Lord Orville is indeed too good to be true, and like all Prince Charmings, I suspect, his extraordinary virtues are not only compensation but justification for the way things are. For it should be clear that the consistent courtliness of Lord Orville tends to justify ruling-class male control and that Lord Orville, as an exemplum of what male authority ought to be, of what Burney wishes to believe it is, provides a counterweight to persons like Sir Clement, whose courtly fictions barely conceal what a landed patriarchal order, in its abuse of women, really felt like.

The remorse of Sir John Belmont, Evelina's real father, is a further endorsement of the landed and patriarchal order, for in contrast to men of the trading classes, who are evidently incapable of reform, Sir John demonstrates at length the inclination and capacity of ruling-class men to take upon themselves the sole responsibility for justice and their own redemption. Having long since recognized the real status of his wife, Caroline—she is not prey but treasure—Sir John ritually humiliates himself in front of Evelina, the "dear resemblance of [her] murdered mother": "behold thy father at thy feet!—bending thus lowly to implore you would not hate him." What is more, Sir John is prepared to share with Evelina the benefits of his social and economic privilege. She is to have birth *and* fortune—an immediate £30,000 and an extra £1,000 "which he insisted that I should receive entirely for my own use, and expend in equipping myself properly for the new rank of life to which I seem destined." Here is another benefit of supporting the landed patriarchy.

There is undeniable zest on Burney's part over Evelina's acquisition of birth and fortune, and her zest is particularly evident because this is the only time in the novel that we know what anyone is worth. But Burney's enthusiasm for Evelina's rise is carefully controlled in the interests of tradition, for as an author she shares little of Austen's or of Richardson's delight in merging the ruling class with persons of the lower orders. It is significant, for example, that Burney tells us only what is bestowed on Evelina by her father and that this rightful fortune, the fortune to which she has been born, is bestowed before her marriage to Lord Orville. The effect is to undermine any emphasis on profit in Evelina's marriage and to guard against any real challenge to the integrity of class divisions. Lord Orville is allowed to find treasure in a woman of small fortune, but that woman is then established as an heiress and the daughter of a baronet. Ultimately, the love plot in this novel represents no dilution of the ruling orders, and, despite Evelina's rise, oligarchy, patriarchy, and the status quo are triumphant. Burney's endorsement of class divisions goes hand in hand with her ultimate endorsement of women's subordination to men.

IV

But *Evelina*, of course, is more than a simple endorsement of patriarchy—as run by gentlemen—and of the ideologies with which it justifies and mitigates its power. It is also the history of a young woman's progress, a form of Erbildungsroman. It is possible to see in Evelina's progress, for example, some reflections of a traditional male quest plot or initiation story. Like many a young man, Evelina enters the world, is initiated into the nature of her society, and, one might argue, grows in prudence and good judgment. For the first two volumes of the novel, in fact, she satirizes male conceit, resists male control, and becomes increasingly skillful at exerting what in this novel is a highly signficant form of power—the power of self-defense, a form of power as autonomy. To a limited degree, in fact, *Evelina* entertains a fantasy of female power which is in some tension with the novel's endorsement and idealization of landed male control. The nature of that autonomy is subtle and it is also deliberately qualified, for Burney feared above all things "ridicule or censure as a female." But, as George Eliot has put it, "yoked creatures" may have their "private opinions," and it is Evelina's private opinions which are the source of what we must call her power in this novel.

Evelina is capable of private opinons because of her extraordinary innocence and inexperience, traditionally feminine qualities which tend to excuse those opinions at the same time that they provide their source. In the myth of Evelina's childhood, she has grown up "naturally" at Berry Hill and has been nurtured in this complete rural isolation by a foster father who is a clergyman and an isolate, a man totally uncorrupted by the privileges of sex and rank. Thus when Evelina enters the world—as represented by London, Bristol, and Howard Grove—she enters with a perfectly unjaundiced eye and an unsullied if modest sense of her own consequence. One form of autonomy which this feminine innocence allows her is the power to resist the humiliating visions of herself which the male community is ready to impose. It is Evelina's private opinion that she is neither merchandise nor prey, and it is primarily her early protection from these distorting notions which assures us that her home-grown consequence will never be impaired.

Evelina's inexperience is also the source of her private opinions about the community itself, for she is the traditional innocent, unused to the manners of the great world and therefore able to observe them from the perspective of what is "natural and right." Since most of her letters in the first two volumes are composed of satiric observations and critical judgments about the presumption and the assaults of men, it is evidently *not* natural or right, from Evelina's point of view, that men should assume superiority to or control over women. Here, for example, is her response to her first assembly: "The gentlemen, as they passed and repassed, looked as if they thought we were quite at their disposal, and only waiting for the honour of their commands; . . . and I thought it so provoking, that I determined in my own mind that, far from humouring such airs, I would rather not dance at all." Satire, it should be noted, is one form of autonomy, and Evelina is a nimble satirist of the presumption and conceit of males.

But Evelina does more than satirize. In her inexperience, she also *acts*—rashly and rebelliously—which is another degree of autonomy altogether. She refuses Lovel, accepts Lord Orville, laughs out loud when Lovel complains, criticizes Sir Clement, and tries to elude him, all because she feels like it, because her natural self-consequence prompts her to act in direct contradiction to the rules of behavior which give men the authority to choose—and the rationale for feeling arrogant—and which give women the right politely to refuse and then only if they are willing to forgo the pleasures of dancing altogether. It is this turn for satire and this impulse to resist which make Evelina powerful and refreshing: she is feminine but not, initially at least, completely passive, and in the guise of innocent response she musters no little resistance to the oppressions and assaults of patriarchy.

Evelina's modest power, however, is in tension with Burney's justification of male ruling-class control and with the ideology that genteel women are really treasure, and this tension is suggested in a variety of defensive strategies, ranging from assurances of Evelina's innocence to qualifications of her autonomy and ultimately to the abandonment of the quest plot altogether. One strategy which prevents the conventional reader from taking umbrage, from leveling censure at Evelina "as a female," is Burney's emphasis upon that innocence and inexperience which prompt Evelina to be satirical and to rebel in the first place. Although we are invited to agree with Evelina as a critical observer, we are also invited to regard her with a fairly patronizing air. She is still a "little rustic," a perceptive little rustic to be sure, but for all her wit she is still a charming, because innocent, country girl. Evelina also confines her satire to letters meant only for her guardian—much as the "silent observant Miss Fanny" confined her satiric strictures to her diary or to correspondence with her sisters and with Daddy Crisp. There can be little protest, after all, about a yoked creature having her own opinions if those opinions are not allowed to circulate freely. Letter writing, as a narrative mode, functions in *Evelina* in a traditionally feminine way: it passes off public criticism as private and therefore innocent remark. Evelina's impulsive actions, however, her breaking of the rules, are quite another thing. They may be satisfying to the reader, but they are officially incorrect, and the nearer they come to being deliberate the more they are criticized. Mr. Villars, for example, forgives Evelina for ignorantly refusing one partner and then accepting another but not for making up a partner to escape Sir Clement: "I am sure I need not say, how much more I was pleased with the mistakes of your inexperience at the private ball, than with the attempted adoption of more fashionable manners at the ridotto. But your confusion and mortifications were such as to entirely silence all reproofs on my part."

Mr. Villars lays a finger here on still another way in which Burney qualifies, and therefore secures toleration for, Evelina's autonomy. Evelina's impulsive resistance to restriction gets her into trouble, succeeds in making *her* feel mortification. Her autonomy in one quarter, moreover, is continually juxtaposed with an ostensibly charming failure of self-control in another. For, if Evelina makes some efforts at self-assertion with Lovel and Sir Clement, she can barely speak to Lord Orville, so awed is she by his superior "manners," "figure," and "rank." It is simply impossible to censure her for being too bold when the kindly attentions of a lord reduce her to hanging her head, looking at her fan, and feeling a fool.

As if this were not enough, Evelina is also made ineffective in asserting herself with gentlemen, even with Lovel, and her ineffectiveness in turn opens the way for male protection. Lord Orville intervenes for her "with some warmth" when Lovel demands an explanation, leads Sir Clement away from her after she has burst into tears, risks a duel to insure her against Lovel's insults in the future, and is given to offering his coach, inquiring after her safety, and expressing general concern for her well-being. These encounters with Lord Orville keep us in touch with the notion that, however charmingly satiric, Evelina still needs someone to protect her, and this is a view of Burney's heroine which is confirmed by the very structure of the novel, for Evelina's narrative letters are regularly interspersed with replies from Mr. Villars. The latter, by always correcting or affirming Evelina's judgments, commending or gently censuring her behavior, reminds us all the while that she is a young woman merely on leave from fatherly supervision and paternal protection.

V

Still, for all the qualification of her powers, Evelina does grow in autonomy and self-control, not with gentlemen, to be sure, but with men of the trading and aspiring classes. Mr. Smith may force her to attend the Hampstead assembly, but he cannot make her dance, for Evelina has learned the rules, and she has also acquired some spirit to use them for her own protection: "the extreme vanity of this man, makes me exert a spirit which I did not, till now, know that I possessed." Eventually she manages such "reserve and coldness" that both Smith and Branghton are persuaded to leave her alone.

The quest plot of this novel, which is partially realized in Evelina's success at finally defending herself against the two men most inclined to see her as merchandise, may be seen as a projection of Burney's vague hankerings for revenge, revenge not on the trading classes, for the view of women as merchandise was not confined in life to the lower orders, but revenge—unthinkingly, confusedly—on the disparaging attitudes toward single women that were much more widely spread. It was unthinkable perhaps for Burney to oppose herself to what actually sustained those attitudes in life: the landed patriarchal order as a whole and specifically the economic contradiction between genteel men and women. It was equally impossible perhaps even to locate the patriarchal order as the source of women's lowered status. Evelina's victory, therfore, is the working out of anger and of a desire for revenge, but of revenge in a sphere where revenge was safe, where it could even be approved of by those with real authority—and Burney's upper-class readers were especially fond of her satires on the vulgarity of the trading orders.

It is also evident from the ease of Evelina's victory that Burney considered the trading orders an easy mark, for in 1778 industrial takeoff, along with the dramatic rise of men in trade, had not yet begun. Men of the trading classes, therefore, may be bested by a woman, while gentlemen cannot because, from Burney's point of view, the former lack social and political consequence. Their awareness of money and of money's relation to status and power may be scorned because there is no conscious danger of its becoming more widespread. And the mercantile vision of women, which they are made to represent, may be summarily dismissed because, in one so committed to courtly ideologies and to males of the ruling class, that vision could not be conceived of as the coming thing.

Evelina, then, is allowed a limited victory with Branghton and Smith, but that is all, for the whole notion of her progress in autonomy and self-defense is in conflict with Burney's idealization of male control, with the courtly fiction that she wishes to sustain, and with the "happy ending" that she must create to secure that fiction for her heroine. The conditions of quest are in conflict with the requirements of marriage and of love. Evelina therefore may acquire a certain skill in fending off assault—no mean accomplishment in this novel—but her responsibility as an adult is not to maintain that ability. Quite the opposite: her destiny is to *be* protected, that is, to marry, and her preparation for this future must be to abdicate rather than to maintain her power. In the third volume, therefore, Evelina moves from the ranks of the trading classes and from the vulgar household of Madame Duval to the upper-class establishment of Mrs. Beaumont, where she feels so ill at ease among her social superiors that she loses all her previous "spirit" and responds to the most flagrant forms of abuse with blushes and silence.

The third volume also marks a shift in the locus of satiric observation. In the first two volumes Evelina is almost alone as a satiric observer, and her eye for the ridiculous makes us feel, despite her ineffectiveness in action and her deference to Lord Orville, that she is still a person of some autonomy and self-control. In the third volume, however, by far the greater share of satirical observation belongs to Mrs. Selwyn, a woman who is witty, effective, and appealing but who is also roundly condemned. Mr. Villars has "often been disgusted at her unmerciful propensity to satire." Sir Clement censures her for the "unbounded license of her tongue"—a quality "intolerable" in a woman—and Evelina, who is surprised at Mrs. Selwyn's "severity," observes that she is both *"masculine"* and wanting in "gentleness." That Mrs. Selwyn is still undeniably attractive to the reader is a measure perhaps of Burney's own ambivalence, for love of the ridiculous was her best quality as a writer; but, whatever its value in a novelist, a turn for satire was hardly a virtue in a bride.

To deprive Evelina of satire, of course, is to deprive her of power. But, since abdication of power is a traditional preparation for marriage, Burney, despite her inner conflicts, continues officially to endorse the status quo. What one senses, then, in the condemnation of Mrs. Selwyn is a preparation for matrimony, an attempt to mitigate our sense that Evelina has been powerful, because satirical, in the first two volumes of the novel. Indeed, the Evelina of the third volume is characterized less by satire than by sentiment, and the imprudent but lively reactions of the first and second volumes give way to the more traditionally sanctioned activities, like the weeping and fainting, of the third. Evelina's discovery of her brother, Mr. Macartney, and her reconciliation with her father provide grand occasions for the display of sentiment while reaffirming the value of family, of family feeling, and in particular of filial affection: Evelina spends a good part of the scene with Belmont at her father's feet and upon her knees.

The end of *Evelina,* then, is marked by a decline in Evelina's autonomy, an autonomy which is in tension not just with matrimony but with landed patriarchy as a whole. The novel's quest plot is dissolved into its love plot, and Evelina must marry. Ideologically, in literature and in life, there is no other "happy ending." Evelina's progress in self-defense must be cut short. Her "progress," in fact, is circular, for her encounter with the world is finally a genteel woman's traditional encounter; it is a time of waiting, a time of transition, during which she is transferred from the protection of one male authority to the protection of another. The entire action of *Evelina* in fact takes place on an extended leave from one guardian and culminates in the acquisition of another, whose nuptial promise is that he will protect her: "then shall it be the sole study of my life to endeavour to soften your past,—and guard you from future misfortunes!" Lord Orville is also closely identified in character with Evelina's guardian. In volume I we are told that Orville's "sweetness, politeness, and diffidence" will ripen into Villars's "benevolence, dignity, and goodness." And in volume 3 Evelina exclaims: "was there ever such another man as Lord Orville?—Yes, *one* other now resides at Berry Hill!" Lord Orville and Reverend Villars: even the names are similar, and at the end of the novel Evelina and Orville return to Villars and to Berry Hill. It is a fitting locus for the end of a journey which has taken her from protected minor to *femme couverte*.

VI

Since Evelina is not responsible for her future, since her destiny is to be protected from rather than to act upon the world, to receive the identity of treasure rather than to create it, we cannot attach to her growth and autonomy the same significance we might attach to the growth and autonomy of a young man. However much we value her wit and rebellious behavior, we must value male authority even more, and Burney, perhaps in compensation for her heroine's decline, devotes much of the last volume to a demonstration of the fact that female power is not enough. Evelina, we will remember, has been reduced to silence and blushes by the affronts of Mrs. Beaumont's guests, when Lord Orville begins to intervene, with increasing frequency, on her behalf. As he continues to intervene, he acquires a series of titles which justify him in the role of protector. In the first two volumes he bears little more than the title of a dance partner, but in the third he moves quickly from friend to brother to lover and ultimately to husband. Each title lends him increasing authority to protect Evelina from the lascivious energies of Lord Merton and Sir Clement.

But the culmination of Lord Orville's intervention and of the novel's justification of ruling-class male control comes in the last episode, in Lord Orville's encounter with Captain Mirvan, who is the ultimate expression of that authority or power to impose oneself which society has fostered in males, especially males of the ruling class. The captain would appear to be the younger son of a country gentleman, the untutored sort for whom a naval commission might be purchased but the sort who remained rude and countrified, although he might marry the daughter of a lady (Mrs. Mirvan is the daughter of Lady Howard). The captain may also represent an earlier and rougher version of the ruling-class male, for Madame Duval calls his rudeness old-fashioned and Mirvan, in contrast to all the younger gentry in the novel, makes no stab whatsoever at seeming courtly. Whatever his heritage, however, Captain Mirvan embodies the most open and most physically brutal expression of male control in the novel, and he is the one man in relation to whom all women are consistently without resources.

Most men in the book impose themselves on women only, whereas Mirvan imposes himself on the world. But his attacks on "unmanly men" suggest that the essence of "manly" power is to him control over women and that men ought to make this control explicit, not disguise or soften it with fictions. Courtliness, from the captain's point of view, is degrading to men and women both: "the men, as they call themselves, are no better than monkeys; and as to the women, why they are mere dolls." To be a real man is to exert force without concealment, and Mirvan as a real man, husband, and father relishes the control he can impose on any woman even vaguely connected with him: "I never suffer anybody to be in a passion in my house, but myself"; "I expect obedience and submission to orders"; "I charge you . . . that you'll never again be so impertinent as to have a taste of your own before my face."

The captain's assaults on Madame Duval, the most physically brutal in the novel, combine two aspects of the landed patriarchy for which he stands—the force which men, especially men of the ruling class, feel authorized to use against women and the force employed by the state, and its feudal representatives, against traditional enemies: the captain first attacks Duval for being French and then pursues his torments, it would appear, because she is a nonsubmissive woman. As a representative of the landed patriarchy, then, Captain Mirvan suggests the mutually reenforcing relation between the control belonging to the head of state, to the paterfamilias, and to the male civilian; and in his brutality he represents the capacity for physical violence which underlies and enforces the control of all three. When verbal insult is insufficient to his feelings, the captain simply attacks Duval physically, seizes her wrists, threatens to throw her from windows, pushes her into puddles, shakes her until she sobs, and ultimately, under cover of a fake robbery, drags her down a road, throws her into a ditch, and ties her to a tree. He is an image of the violence potential in patriarchy, even patriarchy in the hands of gentlemen, and as such he suggests the real necessity for reconciliation to the patriarchal order.

Women in the novel, accordingly, appear almost totally powerless to oppose Mirvan's show of force. Mrs. Mirvan, who at least tries to dissuade Sir Clement when he is pursuing Evelina, does not dare speak to the captain when he is out of humor and attempts little more than distracting him from brutalities when he is in. Maria Mirvan is merely a shadow and suffers in silence while her father makes "rude jests upon the bad shape of her nose." Lady Howard has a "sort of tacit agreement . . . that she should not appear to be acquainted with his schemes." And that the untitled captain disrupts the peace of courtly Howard Grove is a classic example of the extent to which gender outranks class position—even Evelina is intimidated into silence when the captain plays his most brutal tricks on her grandmother, Madame Duval. Burney, moreover, far from disapproving this feminine meekness, appears to endorse and support it, for Madame Duval, the one woman who tries to resist the captain's control, becomes herself an object of satire by abusing the captain's "ill-politeness" in terms which are themselves a study in rudeness and vulgarity. Both the tone and the fact of her resistance are also explained away by her origins. She began life as a "waiting-girl" in a tavern, married above her station, acquired wealth and pretensions to gentility, but remained "uneducated and unprincipled; ungentle in her temper, and unamiable in her manners." Her recalcitrance, therefore, is nothing the novel endorses: only a lower-class woman would meet force with force.

What is more, Duval's assertions of herself against the captain are also ineffective, for he is always the more powerful antagonist. The captain's attacks upon Duval leave her screaming for help, sobbing with passion, crying in pain, and roaring "in the utmost agony of rage and terror." So much for women who resist. None of the other women, either, ever come to her assistance. Lady Howard pretends not to know what is afoot. Evelina is afraid to tell her that the robbery is a fake, and Mrs. Mirvan politely despairs of having any influence whatsoever on her husband's conduct. Bonding between women, it would seem, is futile, and it is finally Sir Clement who, at Evelina's request, puts a momentary end to the captain's brutalities by leaving for London.

The captain then disappears for some 250 pages, but when he is brought back on stage, in the last episode of the novel, he is brought back to demonstrate once again the violence and the force of bad male energies, with the understanding of course that the bad male energies which count are those of gentlemen. Mirvan is also brought back to demonstrate the powerlessness of females, for this is finally what justifies male control in *Evelina*. Real power in this novel, one should note, is actually defined so as to preclude women generally from having their share, for power in *Evelina* is the power of control, the power to impose oneself forcibly upon another or to defend oneself against being forcibly imposed upon. This is not the kind of power which women have ever had much authority or opportunity to use. It is, however, the kind of power which landed men really enjoyed not just in relation to women but in relation to most men who were not of the ruling class, and these landed men supply the model of power in *Evelina*.

It is this power of control and of defense against it which Mirvan and Orville display in the last episode of the novel. The captain has imposed himself upon the company by dressing up a monkey and introducing it as Lovel's relation. The monkey is biting Lovel's ear rather painfully; the captain is laughing; and the frightened ladies are jumping upon their chairs when Lord Orville, "ever humane, generous, and benevolent," flings the monkey from the room and shuts the door. This is Orville's most decisive action in the book—the only time anyone succeeds in containing Mirvan—and what it tells us, once and for all, is something the novel has already taught us: that only good and ruling-class male control is effective against bad, that women's power in particular is not effectual, that female abdication of autonomy is therefore justified, and that in a world demonstrably full of bad male energies the only lasting protection is to marry.

Fathers and Daughters:
The Trauma of Growing Up Female

Mary Poovey

Fanny Burney's first novel, written when she was in her early twenties, and Mary Shelley's last novel, published when Shelley was nearly forty, have few superficial similarities. The sometimes ribald comedy of *Evelina* (1778) provides an obvious contrast to the sentimental, decidedly melodramatic plot of *Falkner* (1837), and the extreme passivity of Burney's heroine highlights even the limited assertiveness of Elizabeth Raby. But in at least one respect the novels do bear a remarkable similarity to each other. In both works, the writers develop their plots so as to introduce the likelihood of what is potentially the most traumatic moment in a young girl's maturation: the clash between her duty towards her father and her affection for a lover. Typically in modern society, girls have tended to remain dependent upon their parents—and, specifically, their fathers—longer than boys, and, for both social and psychological reasons, girls have also tended to fix their affections upon their fathers, as lords in the patriarchal mansion and as necessary replacements for their earlier libidinal attachments to their mothers. Yet at least since the middle of the eighteenth century, as personal preference rather than parents' will has increasingly dictated the choice of a marriage partner, girls have enjoyed at least one moment of theoretical autonomy. The brief period of courtship, the moment at which a woman acquiesces to the imploring suitor or exercises her legitimate "negative," has seemed to signal her independence from her father's will and from her emotional fixation upon

From *Men by Women*, edited by Janet Todd. © 1981 by Holmes & Meier Publishers, Inc.

him. This moment of putative autonomy, then, more than any other, potentially brings the young woman into conflict both with the social imperative that she have only tractable desires and with the psychological necessity that she love her father so as to wrench her libidinal fixation from her mother. In other words, the moment at which a young girl transfers her affection from her father to a lover threatens to create a collision between roles and psychological postures which have been previously mutually exclusive; and the subsequent conflicts—between duty and inclination, between the behavior proper to a daughter and that demanded of an autonomous individual—seem inevitably to mark the threshold of adult identity, to separate the girl from the woman she struggles to become.

The intensity with which Burney and Shelley invest this conflict attests to its significance. Yet what is perhaps most interesting about their depictions is the fact that, despite the trauma of the conflict, both authors avoid exploring its complexities and, in fact, ostentatiously dismiss or repress the potential confrontation before the heroine is required to react to it. Far from suggesting that these writers have successfully resolved this traumatic moment in their heroines' maturation, I think the very fact that they center this dilemma only to avoid it attests to both the anxiety such a conflict arouses and the psychological complexities it uncovers. I want to argue that, for these writers at least, the very threat of such a conflict is sufficiently traumatic to demand first confrontation, then denial. No such conflict can be allowed to materialize, because in their society no adequate social or psychological solution is possible. As the story of Clarissa suggests, a woman who insists upon autonomy in patriarchal society is doomed to live—and die—outside society's protective institutions. Indeed, within the patriarchal family, the very promise of female autonomy is false; for if the daughter chooses a husband, she relegates herself to a second dependency as wife, and if she will not choose, she courts the twin negations of rape and spinsterhood. Moreover, no psychological resolution is possible because, as feminist psychologists have pointed out, the girl's original and ongoing identification with the (socially) inferior mother prevents her from ever really attaining psychological autonomy; her choice of a husband, therefore, demands a second recognition of inferiority, and her transfer of affection can only be a gesture of weakness, not strength. Yet, as a close reading of these two heroines' brush with this dilemma reveals, even within this apparent psychological and social paralysis, opportunities for the exercise of a particularly feminine power do exist. In this essay I want to suggest that the way in which these two women novelists have chosen to characterize and deploy fathers and lovers stems, at least in part, from their desires to remind us of the trauma implicit in this crucial stage of a young girl's life and to point out the forms of power women are, as a consequence, driven to employ.

In *Evelina*, Fanny Burney prepares her reader for this paradigmatic confrontation in three important ways. In the first place, the plot contains not one father but two, and, in the second place, Burney ties her heroine's almost reluctant quest for social maturity to *both* the discovery and reunion with her father *and* Evelina's marriage to Lord Orville. And finally, in the course of the novel Burney provides two prominent examples of confrontations between fathers and lovers, and in each case, the conflict not only causes emotional anguish, but also precipitates the crises that punctuate the central plot. Yet, despite the apparent amassing of circumstantial support, Evelina is spared the emotional turmoil of a conflict between duty and desire. By a last-minute, decidedly awkward contrivance of the plot, Burney effectively decenters the very crisis which she had prepared us to expect. Through what amounts to narrative sleight of hand, Evelina becomes the acknowledged daughter of Sir John Belmont and the wife of Lord Orville in such rapid succession that Evelina has literally no opportunity to suffer an emotional conflict. And, to further defuse this potential crisis, the lover who ushers Evelina into a new set of roles and responsibilities is more like a father to her than is the real father she has so recently found.

At the outset of the novel, Burney reveals that her heroine's "situation" is especially "cruel." For, although Evelina is being raised by a kindly old country clergyman, Reverend Villars, she is actually the only child of the wealthy Sir John Belmont. Because Belmont was not able to secure the fortune he had hoped to win through marriage, he has disavowed both the marriage and the child who should rightfully inherit his estate. Now motherless, fatherless, innocent, and strikingly beautiful, the young Evelina is being raised to confine her expectations and desires to the limited possibilities of Berry Hill.

Yet as a maturing young woman, Evelina soon betrays wishes that are considerably less tractable than Villars had hoped to encourage. Burney depicts the gradual awakening of Evelina's independent desires (which are still not quite desires for independence) as a phenomenon completely beyond her control and conscious will. Yet even if the thought of visiting London is originally only a response to the prompting of her temporary hostess, Lady Howard, Evelina soon discovers in herself a capacity for imagining—and thus desiring—life outside the protective Berry Hill. "My dear Sir," Evelina begins her letter to Villars, "I am desired to make a request to you. . . . Lady Howard insists upon my writing!—yet I hardly know how to go on; a petition implies a want and have you left me one? No, indeed." Even casting herself as the grammatical object of her sentences, however, cannot keep her a child forever. Evelina is as "innocent as an angel, and artless as purity itself," yet as she details the sights of London, her pen acquires a voice of its own and dictates the desire she wants to repress.

> They tell me that London is now in full splendour. Two playhouses are open,—the Opera-house,—Ranelagh,—and the Pantheon.—You see I have learned all their names. However, pray don't suppose that I make any point of going, for I shall hardly sigh, to see them depart without me, though I shall probably never meet with such another opportunity. And, indeed, their domestic happiness will be so great,—it is natural to wish to partake of it.
>
> I believe I am bewitched! I made a resolution, when I began, that I would not be urgent; but my pen—or rather my thoughts, will not suffer me to keep it—for I acknowledge, I must acknowledge, I cannot help wishing for your permission.

Reverend Villars is anxious to keep Evelina at Berry Hill partly because he fears the unscrupulous attention of London rogues. Not wealthy enough to attract an honorable suitor, Evelina is too beautiful to go unnoticed. But Villars's anxiety centers more obsessively on Evelina's desires than on London's dangers. For even though her wish to visit London sneaks in by way of the legitimate longing to experience domestic joy, Villars knows that other wishes will soon follow. "A youthful mind is seldom totally free from ambition," he worries, and "the natural vivacity of [Evelina's] disposition," the "liveliness of [her] fancy," make her especially susceptible to a dangerous elevation of hope and desire. Once outside the paternal home, anything could happen; but what does happen both realizes and surpasses Villars's fears. Evelina *is* accosted by a London rogue, and she *does* meet the man who will carry her away from Villars's side. Even so, Evelina's "natural vivacity" and "lively fancy" remain largely dormant until she encounters the one man who proves a real threat to Villars's position—her real father, Sir John Belmont.

The very thought of asking her long-lost father for recognition—and the social position that would accompany it—catapults Evelina into a paroxysm of competing emotions. "My imagination changes the scene perpetually," Evelina confesses to Villars:

> One moment, I am embraced by a kind and relenting parent, who takes me to that heart from which I have hitherto been banished, and supplicates, through me, peace and forgiveness from the ashes of my mother!—at another, he regards me with detestation, considers me as the living image of an injured saint, and repulses me with horror!

It is important to note here that both Evelina's fantasy and her nightmare entail the heroine's virtual transparency. In both imagined reunions, Evelina simply stands for her deceased mother. The mother's priority in Evelina's imagination suggests both the insignificance the daughter believes herself to possess and the position that Evelina unconsciously wishes to attain. The overtones of a longed-for libidinal relationship with her father clearly surface here, but perhaps equally telling is Evelina's vision of the nature and source of the power she might exercise over her father: as even a feeble substitute for her mother, the young girl is justified in imagining herself punishing her father for his transgression. Evelina does not act on her own—she is only the representative of her mother—nor does she act for herself; indeed, she can barely be accused of acting at all. Yet through the apparently insignificant daughter, the mother is vindicated, and both wronged women imaginatively triumph.

When Evelina eventually confronts Sir John Belmont in person, her emotion surpasses even the agitation she had envisioned. "Almost senseless with terror" at the thought of meeting Belmont, Evelina cannot brave the first sight of him: "an involuntary scream escaped me, and, covering my face with my hands, I sunk on the floor." Beside such agitation, Evelina's emotion for Lord Orville, the decorous lover too unimaginable for Burney even to assign him a Christian name, occasions the merest tremor. At the height of her emotional response to Orville, Evelina's "natural vivacity" once more threatens to overwhelm consciousness: "I scarce breathed; I doubted if I existed,—the blood forsook my cheeks, and my feet refused to sustain me." Yet rather than elaborating this climactic moment, Burney chooses simply to summarize indirectly Evelina's putatively rapturous assent: "in short, my dear Sir, I was not proof against his solicitations—and he drew from me the most sacred secret of my heart!" and to move immediately to the dilemma that has preoccupied Evelina all along—the question of her father(s). In response to Orville's desire to solicit her guardian's blessing, Evelina reveals with evident agitation her deepest anguish: "my Lord," she gasps, "I hardly know myself to whom I most belong."

The theme of a daughter "belonging" to her father has already been introduced twice in *Evelina*, and, although we are only provided indirect perspectives on these situations, the emotional anguish from them permeates the main plot. Both Evelina's mother and brother have, in fact, suffered from the conflict between a daughter's filial duty and her personal inclination. For Miss Evelyn, Evelina's mother, the confrontation centered explicitly on her right to exercise her independent will in choosing a husband. Denied this right, Miss Evelyn eloped with the scheming profligate, Belmont, thus invoking her stepfather's wrath and then the husband's vengeance which has so affected her daughter's life. For Macartney, Evelina's half-brother, the tyranny of a father nearly occasions even more disastrous consequences. His secret courtship of a young Englishwoman in Paris is discovered by the furious father, who entertains respect neither for the preference of his daughter nor for this penniless youth from Scotland. Unable to bear the abuse the raging father heaps upon him, Macartney draws his sword and wounds the tyrannical parent. Burney subsequently underscores the severity of Macartney's forcible violation of the filial bond by allowing him—and the reader—to realize that the man he has wounded is his *own* father. Haunted by guilt, loneliness, and poverty, Macartney is driven to the twin temptations of crime and suicide before Evelina's fortuitous intervention saves him.

In neither of these situations is the reader directly presented with the daughter's emotional turmoil: Evelina's mother is already dead when the story opens and the woman whom Macartney loves remains a peripheral character throughout the novel. Nor is the eminently eligible Orville in any danger of provoking either father to actual disapproval. But the very repetition of this pattern focuses our attention more sharply on the emotional dilemma that seems to threaten Evelina. To marry Orville, after all, will require leaving both her *"more than father,"* Reverend Villars, and her newfound father, Sir John

Belmont. In order to avoid the psychological trauma inherent in this dilemma, the intense emotion Evelina has exhibited throughout the novel toward both fathers must somehow be transferred to Lord Orville. Burney effects this transfer by a complicated series of plot contrivances. First, she separates Evelina from both her fathers, isolating her by calling attention to the intricate situation that has developed around her: because Macartney has finally been granted permission to marry the girl whom Belmont mistakenly believed was his daughter, Evelina cannot join her new father and thus publicly expose her future sister-in-law as a washerwoman's daughter; and because Evelina must soon be accepted as Sir John Belmont's legitimate daughter and heir, she cannot return to Berry Hill and her guardian Villars. Although even Evelina seems embarrassed by the ostentatiousness of this contrivance, she agrees to a double marriage in which she will not be "given away" by either of her fathers. Thus Evelina is metaphorically orphaned, and marriage to Orville, instead of removing her from any father's house, provides a desperately needed home. Moreover, for all intents and purposes, both Evelina's fathers "die" so as to give way to Orville. Belmont, distraught by the emotion his newfound daughter occasions, hurries away from Evelina despite her pleas and tears. And Villars, until this point apparently healthy, suddenly depicts himself as nearing the grave. Praying only that "the weak and aged frame of thy almost idolizing parent" be able to "survive" one last meeting with Evelina, Villars looks forward only to the "ultimate consolation of pouring forth [his] dying words in blessings on [his] child!—closing [his] joy-streaming eyes in her presence, and breathing [his] last faint sighs in her loved arms!"

The transfer of Evelina's emotions is even further facilitated by Burney's characterization of Lord Orville. Evelina rarely discusses Orville's appeal—partly because for much of the novel she remains unaware of her growing affection for him and partly because most of her letters are written to the very man who most dreads losing his "daughter," Reverend Villars. Therefore, apart from Orville's exemplary manners and his ability to appear whenever needed, the reader is given little impression of Evelina's preferred lover. Significantly, however, in the one passage in which Evelina does allow herself to fantasize about Orville, she imagines him not as the young and virile lover he presumably is but as the paternal figure he will eventually become. Evelina's unconscious wishes surface, of course, only when she momentarily believes she no longer has a chance of marrying Orville.

Since the lover no longer arouses unconscionable desire, Evelina pours out her heart to Villars:

> Once, indeed, I thought there existed another,—who, when *time had wintered o're his locks*, would have shone forth among his fellow-creatures with the same brightness of worth which dignifies my honoured Mr. Villars; a brightness how superior in value to that which results from mere quickness of parts, wit, or imagination!

Although Evelina's wedding announcement ("All is over . . . and the fate of your Evelina is decided!") stresses the end of her role as daughter rather than the inauguration of her wifely role, the end of the novel suggests that little has really changed. Returning to Berry Hill and "the arms of the best of men" on her honeymoon trip, Evelina seems only to have expanded her array of fathers; now she "belongs" to them all.

Before this neat resolution, however, Burney does afford the reader one glimpse of the power inherent in the daughter's position. In the penultimate episode of the novel, when Evelina and her long-lost father actually meet, Evelina's earlier fantasy comes true. As "representative of the most injured of women," the daughter momentarily has the upper hand. Despite her conventional protestations of horror at Belmont's debasement, Evelina serves as the agent for both humbling and punishing her father. Speaking in the "name" and with the face of her mother, Evelina momentarily resolves the triangular relationship of father/mother/daughter into a simpler configuration. The intensity with which Burney imagines this scene is unmistakable:

> "Come hither, Evelina: Gracious Heaven! (looking earnestly at me) never was likeness more striking!—the eyes—the face—the form—Oh, my child, my child!" Imagine, Sir, —for I can never describe my feelings, when I saw him sink upon his knees before me! "Oh, dear resemblance of thy murdered mother!—Oh, all that remains of the most injured of women! behold thy father at thy feet!—bending thus lowly to implore you would not hate him. —Oh, then, thou representative of my departed wife, speak to me in her name, and say that the remorse which tears my soul tortures me not in vain!"

Evelina's dream come true is remarkable largely because the daughter once more takes the place of the mother in an emotionally charged encounter with the father. Not only do the overtones of incest resonate here (recalling those with which Burney invested Macartney's encounter with his father), but the very elevation Evelina receives seems charged with significance. Evelina is never so vividly presented as an autonomous, powerful individual as in this moment when—through no design of her own—she stands in for her wronged mother. In fact, as her father prostrates himself before Evelina he is essentially reducing himself to a childish position of helplessness and supplication. If Evelina does not quite become reproving mother to a wayward child, she does borrow power from the authority only mothers are traditionally granted. And, even more important, in her reluctant—but effective—triumph over her father, Evelina indirectly retaliates for the male's crimes against both her mother and herself. Both Evelina and her mother are avenged without having to represent themselves, for, as the image of her mother, Evelina stands for both women without really acting as either one.

The coincidences in the biographies of Fanny Burney and Mary Shelley no doubt help account for the thematic similarities I have identified. Both writers lost their mothers at an early age; both professed to have "excessive," almost romantic attachments to their fathers, yet both women demonstrated anxiety (if not resentment) about the authority their fathers exercised; both women suffered the tyranny of deeply resented stepmothers; and both departed from the typical pattern when they married (Mary Godwin Shelley defied her father and eloped with a married man when she was only fifteen, and Burney did not marry until she was forty-one, choosing then an older, impoverished Frenchman of whom her father expressly disapproved). I want to suggest, however, that beyond these biographical coincidences, at least two other factors help shape the similarities in the latent plots of *Evelina* and *Falkner*. First of all, the triangular configuration which lurks within both daughter's relationships with their fathers duplicates a paradigmatic situation discussed first by Freud and, more recently, by feminist revisionist critics. And secondly, the indirect female power these two women introduce suggests both the limitations imposed upon women by patriarchal society and the ways in which opportunities for self-assertion have been exploited. While these factors may not fully "explain" the implicit or explicit preoccupations of these novels, I think they do help clarify the complexities that haunt these novels' resolutions.

The psychological paradigm seems to me helpful in explaining both the emotional intensity aroused by the confrontation of father and lover and the vestiges of the mother that seem to haunt it. According to Freud's fundamental theory, this moment—the transfer of a female's primary attachment from her father to a (male) lover—is the structural equivalent to the male's resolution of the oedipal complex. But late in his life, Freud acknowledged that because of the variations gender causes in the oedipal pattern, a girl neither experiences nor "resolves" this configuration in the same way as a boy does. And it is these differences—appearing in novels long before Freud or his recent revisionists—that characterize the resolutions of *Evelina* and *Falkner*.

Contemporary versions of the oedipal story emphasize that for children of both sexes, the child's initial—and, in many ways, formative—relationship is with the mother. From the child's primary identification with the mother s/he ideally receives both ego reinforcement and the immediate satisfaction of physical and emotional needs that constitutes the basis of later intimations of perfect fulfillment. For the male child, the critical moment of maturation occurs when this original heterosexual bond is threatened by the intervention of the rival father. In order to avoid confrontation with the stronger father, the boy represses his attachment to his mother and, in the "resolution" which is the basis of patriarchal society, transfers his identification from his mother to his father. Identifying with his father assures the boy that he can eventually form another primary relationship with someone *like* his mother and thus protects him from traumatic loss. For the male child, then, the development of personal autonomy is at least theoretically possible; maturation is a relatively continuous process, marked primarily by the intervention of the father, which, paradoxically, first deprives the boy of power, then gives it back to him through the male's (superior) position in patriarchal society. The male's social and psychological maturation is not an achievement of complete autonomy, however: because his mature heterosexual love is derived from—and retains vestiges of—his original love for his mother, the man is still susceptible to the influence of a maternal figure. Both Burney and Shelley are aware of this susceptibility, and the form of female power they imagine exploits it.

For the girl, on the other hand, the promise of even qualified autonomy does not accompany the oedipal situation. Like the boy, the girl originally identifies with the mother, but for her this is a *preoedipal* identification, more formative and long-lived than the boy's identification. Within this primary relationship the girl confronts the most basic psychic issues—of identity and love, dependence and separation—without the threat of an aggressive competitor. According to Nancy Chodorow's revision of Freud, the girl's first consciousness of the father might promise liberation from, but poses no lasting threat to, her relationship with the mother. Indeed, in order to achieve autonomy, the girl would need to identify with the father more than she is psychically able to:

> When a girl's father does become an important primary person, it is in the context of a bisexual relational triangle. A girl's relation to him is emotionally in reaction to, interwoven and competing with, her relation to her mother. A girl usually turns to her father as an object of primary interest from the exclusivity of the relationship to her mother, but this libidinal turning to her father does not substitute for her attachment to her mother. Instead, a girl retains her preoedipal tie to her mother . . . and builds oedipal attachments to both her mother and father upon it.

Because the girl does not identify with the father, because, indeed, she does not even transfer her affection completely to him, she never achieves psychological autonomy. The identification with the (socially) weak mother remains dominant and the girl never develops the strong superego that would enable her to free herself from her original dependence. Moreover, the moment at which a girl transfers her love from her father to a lover necessitates a second identification with her mother, thus reinforcing, rather than qualifying, the girl's sense of her own inferiority.

What should be a moment of social autonomy for a girl is therefore not really one at all. Indeed, far from allowing the expression of autonomous desire, this moment brings to the surface the complex facets of the girl's psychological immaturity. The promise of social autonomy is in fact false: as wife, the young woman will be as dependent as she was as daughter. Nevertheless, the demands of the situation are real; the moment of choice dictates that the woman take the initiative—or at least the responsibility—for rejecting her father and installing another man in his place. The consequence of these demands—in the face of the girl's inability to meet them—is the exposure of two critical truths of the female situation: the girl sees that her relationship with her father has been largely idealized; and she intuits, however dimly, that the man she has idealized is, in fact, the tyrant of patriarchal society. For Fanny Burney and Mary Shelley, these truths both delimit the opportunities for female self-expression and constitute the foundation for woman's power.

The reasons for a girl's idealization of the father, Nancy Chodorow suggests, involve both his general inaccessibility and the strength of her libidinal attachment to her mother. In patriarchal society, men are typically not responsible for childcare; hence, the physical remoteness of the father allows the girl to project onto him the illusion that he is capable of satisfying those needs which only the mother can really fulfill. This illusion is necessary for the girl even partially to disengage herself from her dependence on and identification with the mother. The young girl, Chodorow explains,

> (and the woman she becomes) is willing to deny her father's limitations (and those of her lover or husband) as long as she feels loved. She is more able to do this because his distance means that she does not really know him. The relationship, then, because of the father's distance and importance to her, occurs largely as fantasy and idealization, and lacks the grounded reality which a boy's relation to his mother has.

In both novels I have examined, the motherless daughters' relationships with the fathers have carried the burden of needs originally and ideally satisfied by the mothers; in a sense, in each novel the relationship with the father is only an imaginative substitute for the absent relationship with the mother. But the young girls cannot recognize this deception until they have sufficient psychological security to risk the loss of their idealized versions of the father—until, that is, another idealized male stands ready to replace him. Thus both Fanny Burney and Mary Shelley characterize the awakening of the daughter's romantic desire as the action which precipitates confrontation with the father. For both, then, the central confrontation is not between the father and the lover, but between the father and the daughter—or, more precisely, between the daughter's idealized version of the father and the other version of him she now sees.

The "other version" of the father is virtually the opposite of the idealized protector the young girl had imagined. The "real" father, these novelists suggest, is passionate, willful, and hence the destroyer of the mother whose self-denying love was powerless before him. As guardian of patriarchal society, then, the father is the tyrant who blocks a woman's social and psychological autonomy, who destroys domestic tranquility, and who reduces both mother and daughter to "cyphers" within the home that should shelter them. The ambivalence this revelation may awaken toward the father may then surface as anger, resentment, or an excessive and compensatory fidelity.

Even within the woman's position of inferiority and dependence, however, both Burney and Shelley locate sources and resources of power—an effective and acceptable means, that is, of expressing their characters' resentment and desires. For as the heroines discover the true nature of their fathers, they also discover their own legitimate social office; as "representatives" of their mothers, they are to carry out the maternal role, they are to civilize and socialize these passionate men. The expression of their anger, like that of desire, must be indirect, but acting as mothers affords these women both the satisfaction of retaliation against the fathers and the comfort of doing their social duty. The expression of these unconscionable wishes, of course, entails the illusion—although not the reality—of self-effacement. Thus, in both novels, the punishment of the father is exacted on behalf of the wronged mother, not of the self. Moreover, in each case, the father openly acknowledges his guilt; the daughter does not have to accuse him, for the father interprets the daughter's mere presence as the sign of punishment deserved. The anger behind the daughter's revenge is therefore displaced, as is the desire to punish; neither Evelina nor Elizabeth consciously wants or tries to punish her father, yet because they are seen as taking the place of their wronged mothers (through physical resemblance or emotional identification), their very presence pricks male conscience and thus initiates the punishment the daughters unconsciously desire. Finally, both Burney and Shelley further mediate this confrontation by displacing the parental relations involved. In *Evelina*, because the kindly Reverend Villars is the idealized father who is replaced by the passionate Sir John Belmont, no conflict develops between Evelina's two versions of her father. And in *Falkner*, both the wronged mother and the passionate father are surrogates for Elizabeth's biological parents. Thus no explicit oedipal conflict need occur; the indirect expression of power legitimate for a female can effectively articulate—and disguise—desire.

While the psychological paradigm I have outlined here is fundamental in accounting for the anger and indirection which characterize the relationship between daughters and fathers in these novels, it is also important to remember that the paradigm acquires this particular character from women's place in patriarchal society. For only because fathers remain idealized figures demanding authority as well as love, and only because women must express—even experience—autonomous desire indirectly, does the female response to fathers and lovers include such disguise and contradiction. Perhaps the tensions implicit in this response are particularly conspicuous in women's novels during the late eighteenth and early nineteenth centuries because this was a period of particular conflict in the expectations generated for women. During these decades, the relatively recent possibility of a woman's choosing her own husband rather than acceding to her father's command was reinforced by innumerable celebrations of "romantic" love; but at the same time, the emergence of what would eventually be called the "Victorian" idealization of woman as a creature wholly without desire made it increasingly difficult for a woman even to recognize, much less express, autonomous desire. Yet even in such periods of social and psychological restrictions, female desire does grow and find its outlet. The fact that in these novels it twists so oddly about the father attests both to its responsiveness to cultural pressures and to its creative, indomitable power.

Privacy and Anonymity in *Evelina*

Jennifer A. Wagner

Evelina is a novel that examines the interplay between the public and the private—public and private spaces, public and private opinion, and particularly the title character's tense and problematic experience of physical and emotional privacy. The brutality of Richardson's *Clarissa,* an obvious precursor, is precisely society's denial of *any* right of possession or privacy whatsoever to that unfortunate young lady. The interest of *Evelina* is in its heroine's subtle strategies to preserve her identity by evading societal demands upon her privacy. The fact that her identity is so problematic—that she does not know, quite literally, who she is and even has a made-up name—provides both the context for the privacy problem and the solution to it: Evelina's very anonymity becomes a powerful screen from society's demands on her integrity and will.

Evelina's lack of identity is figured by her lack of voice at the opening of the novel. There is a certain blankness about Evelina in the first seven letters; we only hear *about* her and hear nothing in her own voice. That blankness might also be indicated by the fact that her assigned pseudonym—Anville—is a sort of mirror image of her first name. But it is important to note that this self-reflexive name reflects her *social* anonymity; as long as Evelina "belongs" to "no one," Villars at least gives her a label that contains that part of her name that *does* belong exclusively to her.

Significantly, however, that new last name is also nearly an ana-

---

gram of Villars's own. And indeed in Evelina's first letters, we see that she regards herself as a cipher of paternal authority. In writing him about the Mirvans' request that she accompany them to London, she displays a tension between what others ask of her, what she wants for herself, and what she knows Villars wants. She would insist that the latter two desires are the same: "A petition implies a want and have you left me one? No indeed." And later, "I have no happiness or sorrow, no hope or fear, but what your kindness bestows."

But this same letter reveals her own desires—as Villars recognizes: "While I am yet in suspense," she writes, "perhaps I may *hope*; but I am most certain that when you have once determined I shall not repine." Evelina haltingly but emphatically closes this first letter with a promise of acquiescence—and an implicit challenge: "Yet I hope—I hope you will be able to permit me to go!" Furthermore, she signs her name "Evelina————"—a disavowal of the name her "most beloved father" has given her, thereby, unintentionally, disavowing his absolute claim on her. "I cannot to *you* sign ANVILLE, and what other name may I claim?" Evelina herself pinpoints the most perplexing aspect of her person, and that aspect that most perplexes those she will soon meet—her anonymity. As she herself observes in her next, Letter 10, "As to me, I should be alike unknown in the most conspicuous or most private part of the house."

As this passage suggests, one of the most important ways Burney thematizes the tension between the private and the public in her novel is by 'contrasting private and public spaces, examining how behavior and expectations vary in each. In this *Evelina* clearly resembles *Clarissa*, a primary precursor text, although private spaces are rarely threatened in *Evelina* in the horrific manner of both *Clarissa* and *Pamela*. Evelina has available at *all* times her "own room," where she indulges her feelings in her letters to Villars. The letters are a sort of private, textual space that contrasts with the public spaces where one must "publish" oneself and one's intentions. Particularly toward the end of the novel, as the heroine becomes more and more aware of her own private romantic feelings *as* such, "my own room" is mentioned more and more frequently. Like Berry Hill, "my own room" is also a place of retirement where society can be viewed (in letters) with a candid, critical eye or altogether ignored.

It is not quite accurate, however, to say these places of retirement are equally private. Berry Hill is represented as an idyllic place, and so it is for Evelina as long as she is a child, as long as her identity is subsumed by Villars's own. Once she leaves Berry Hill, however, the Villars-Anville equation never again truly exists. It is indeed significant that the reader becomes more aware of Evelina's retirement to "her own room" in the novel; she claims this space emphatically as property, with strong boundaries, set apart even from Villars himself. And, indeed, along with Willoughby and Orville, there is no one so intrusive to Evelina's privacy as Villars himself, after her return to Berry Hill.

In contrast to Berry Hill and "my own room" are the many public places to which Evelina is introduced; generally, "the world," more specifically, London (with its dances, assemblies, parks, theaters), Bristol Hotwells, and Bath. It is simply the public nature of these places that initially impresses the heroine: "We passed a most extraordinary evening. A *private* ball this was called, so I expected to have seen about four or five couple; but Lord! my dear sir, I believe I saw half the world!" (Letter 11). When Orville first asks her to dance, she registers her fear of strangers—"I could not see one person that I knew" (Letter 11)—and also her ignorance of so-called "public places":

> When he found this, he changed the subject, and talked of public places and public performers; but he soon discovered that I was totally ignorant of them.
> He then, very ingeniously, turned the discourse to the amusements and occupations of the country.
>
> (Letter 11)

What mortifies Evelina here, though, is her realization that between the first and second dances Orville has tried to identify her:

> He was satisfied, I suppose, with his former successless efforts to draw me out or, rather, I fancied he had been inquiring *who I was*. This again disconcerted me; and the spirits I had determined to exert, again failed me.
>
> (Letter 10)

This discomfiture is aggravated when she learns of a conversation concerning her ill manners, in which Lovel notes that "really, for a person who is nobody, to give herself such airs,—I own I could not command my passion. For, my Lord, though I have made diligent inquiry—I cannot learn who she is" (Letter 12).

Her problems only worsen when, in an effort to defend herself from the intrusiveness of Willoughby, she "usurps," as it were, Orville's name: "Make use of his name!—what impertinence—he can never know how it happened,—he can only imagine it was from an excess of vanity;—well, however, I shall leave this bad city to-morrow, and never again will I enter it" (Letter 13). She is quickly learning that social status depends to an extreme degree on one's name, and, more important perhaps from her standpoint, that the assumption of a man's name is a woman's best form of protection. In this society a woman must, it seems, "belong" to someone—either to a father and his lineage, to a husband or even, temporarily, to a dancing partner.

A similar fear of being named is evident much later at Bristol Hotwells, where once discovered ("Where can you so long have hid yourself?") she tells with undisguised horror of being publicly identified as the subject of a set of verses:

> We went first to the pump-room. It was full of company; and the moment we entered, I heard a murmuring of *"That's she!"* and, to my great confusion, I saw every eye turned towards me. I pulled my hat over my face, and, by the assistance of Mrs. Selwyn, endeavoured to screen myself from observation, nevertheless, I found I was so much the object of general attention, that I entreated her to hasten away.
>
> (Letter 72)

Adds Willoughby soon after this, "Yours was the first name I heard at the pump-room. But had I *not* heard your name, such a description could have painted no one else."

In these scenes Evelina plays with a potent form of defense—just that anonymity that she herself and nearly everyone else seeks to puncture. Anonymity in this novel is something like a power vacuum that must be filled; note the curiosity her lack of identity excites. In a society that so values the name, anonymity can be turned into a real weapon. Lovel's perplexity regarding her name and status probably preserves her from the full brunt of his obnoxiousness—particularly as Evelina slips behind the authority of Orville's name. Furthermore, her anonymity also aids her at that first assembly because no one knows what they *should* expect from her, hence temporarily short-circuiting the charge of possible ill-conduct on her part.

One of Evelina's methods of preserving her anonymity is by maintaining silence; besides simply being shy, Evelina's silence is also a form of protection, for speech in this novel is clearly a powerful social tool and weapon in its own right, used to pry information from its members. One's manner of speech becomes a fast way of "identifying" persons.

The problem of social anonymity dovetails with the problem of Evelina's literal anonymity. Lady Howard assures Villars that London will be a safe place for Evelina, precisely because if Madame Duval did cross Evelina's path, she would not recognize Evelina's pseudonym; that is, the immensity of London ensures her anonymity. (The same mistaken expectation of anonymity leads Clarissa and Anna Howe to place Clarissa's escape there.) The thematic paradox here however is that Evelina originally goes to London precisely to *be* exposed to society.

Once discovered by Madame Duval and the Branghtons, she is taken in and taken over, and anonymity in the public sphere takes on an even more crucial role—as defense from the ridicule of those who must associate Evelina with her ignorant and ill-mannered relations: "I am sure I shall not be very ambitious of being known to any more of my relations, if they have any resemblance to those whose acquaintance I have been introduced to already" (Letter 17). Her desire to remain anonymous in London is "betrayed" by both her own and Mrs. Mirvan's surprise. But that desire also reflects her social snobbery, as she accompanies the Branghtons to those same public places she attended among more genteel company:

> Indeed, he [Captain Branghton] laughs and talks so terribly loud in public, that he frequently makes us ashamed of belonging to him.
>
> (Letter 19)

> I then found that his aim was to discover the nature of her connection with me; but I felt so much ashamed of my near relationship to her, that I could not persuade myself to answer him.
>
> (Letter 21)

And for a final of many possible examples:

> While we were strolling round the garden, I perceived, walking with a party of ladies at some distance, Lord Orville! I instantly retreated behind Miss Branghton, and kept out of sight till we had again passed him; for I dreaded being

seen by him again in a public walk with a party of which I
was ashamed.

(Letter 54)

In these scenes, Evelina is always "fearing to be known," and soon
after the passage quoted above, Evelina unwisely "whispered Miss
Branghton not to speak my name."

Obscurity, or anonymity, though worthless and undesirable socially, is at this point devoutly to be wished by Evelina; her anonym,
Anville, has been rendered less than useless, indeed harmful, as the
Orville/Willoughby contingents learn of her relation to the socially
inferior Branghtons. Anonymity is a kind of concealment, a social
camouflage that she uses even against Orville, whose curiosity concerning Macartney toward the end of the novel Evelina resists by
refusing to name their relation and by insisting on her privacy despite
her growing intimacy with Orville.

Privacy is a sort of "self-ownership" that society inherently and to
a greater or lesser degree threatens. The novel demonstrates this concept by focusing on Evelina's lack of *literal* identity and the problem of
"ownership," both literal and figurative. Duval forces the identity
issue by suggesting a legal effort to reclaim Evelina's inheritance, or
what properly (and property) belongs to her; this of course is the *literal*
question of ownership. Lady Howard's letter to Villars just after this,
however, makes the "ownership" problem a more subtle one:

> Surely Sir John Belmont, wretch as he has shown himself,
> could never see his accomplished daughter, and not be proud
> to own her, and eager to secure her the inheritance of his
> fortune. The admiration she met with in town, though
> merely the effect of her external attractions, was such, that
> Mrs. Mirvan assures me, she would have had the most
> splendid offers, had there not seemed to be some mystery in
> regard to her birth, which, she was well informed was
> assiduously, though vainly, endeavoured to be discovered.
>
> (Letter 27)

The word "own" here carries a primary sense of "to acknowledge"
—but interestingly, the word clearly brings to mind the sense "to
possess" as well. This double sense resurfaces in Lady Howard's letter
to Sir John Belmont himself: "To be owned *properly* by you is the first
wish of her heart" (Letter 31). Her identification as a Belmont de-

mands an acknowledgment and a claim to ownership, both on Evelina's part and on Sir John's. Just as Evelina was required to accept the protection of a male figure in the social context, so here does society demand she be "owned" before she can have a place in it.

Evelina herself participates in this network of linguistic connections:

> I took my usual place, and Mrs. Beaumont, Lady Louisa, and Mrs. Selwyn, entered into their usual conversation. —Not so your Evelina: disregarded, silent, and melancholy, she sat like a cypher, whom, to nobody belonging, by nobody was noticed.
>
> (Letter 75)

Here Evelina pinpoints the relationship between identity, name, acknowledgment, and possession—and shows us too that anonymity and privacy carry a severe price—obscurity. As she complains soon after to Lord Orville, "I hardly know, my Lord, I hardly know myself to whom I most belong" (Letter 76).

But Evelina adds yet another connotation to the word "belong" and to the concept of possession: the connotation of romance. "I now retrace the remembrance of rather as belonging to an object of ideal perfection, formed by my own imagination, than to a being of the same race and nature as those with whom I at present converse" (Letter 41). Orville is a private vision, her own vision, not a partner assigned by someone else. Even Villars's explicit disapproval of Orville (however misguided at the time) has only temporary influence on her feelings.

Evelina's recognition of these private emotions, coinciding with her unhappy return to Berry Hill, is a turning point in the novel, marked by the only block of letters from Evelina *not* addressed to Villars. This set (Letters 57 to 61) is to Maria Mirvan, whom Evelina called earlier "my second self," one who "neither hopes nor fears but as I do" (Letter 26)—as if she were really writing not to another but to herself. These letters, the most "private" and subjective of them all, are not meant for Villars; indeed they are largely a description of her reluctance to reveal to Villars her affection for Orville, lest he attempt to "dispossess" her of that affection. As she openly admits to Maria:

> Every hour I regret the secrecy I have observed with my beloved Mr. Villars; I know not what bewitched me, but I felt at first a repugnance to publishing this affair that I could

not surmount;—and now, I am ashamed of confessing that
I have any thing to confess!

(Letter 59)

The terms of privacy and public exposure are still here—but they
convey now not the question of her familial identity, but her emotional identity.

Evelina is developing a new "private space" in this block of letters
to Maria, a textual privacy of a journal. It is only here, where she
writes to her "second self," that her most private thoughts reveal
themselves; in Letter 57, Evelina "blush[es] for what I have written"
—because it is a revelation of her actual emotional state. Though she
seems to be "not herself" she ends this letter with the interesting
assertion that her heart "never was, never can be, more assuredly *her
own* than at this moment." At the same time, she becomes particularly
aware of her medium as, first of all, an expression or even "replace-
ment" of herself: "My sweet Maria will be much surprised . . . when,
instead of her friend, she receives this letter;—this cold, this inanimate
letter, which will but ill express the feeling of the heart which indites
it" (Letter 57). She is thus more aware of the manner in which writing
both conceals or is inadequate ("I cannot journalize, cannot arrange my
ideas into order"), and reveals true emotion ("I blush for what I have
written"). Furthermore, she begins to see *herself as* a readable text,
whose face and actions publish emotions even as she tries to conceal
them:

> I started from my reverie, and, hardly knowing what I said,
> asked if he had been reading?
>   He paused a moment, and then replied, "Yes, my child;—a
> book that both afflicts and perplexes me."
>   He means *me*, thought I; and therefore I made no answer.
>   "What if we read it together?" continued he, "will you
> assist me to clear its obscurity?"
>
> (Letter 60)

Villars is a competent reader here; a reader of the heart, rather
than the words. Evelina must later urge her natural father to be the
same: "Oh, Sir, . . . that you could but read my heart!" (Letter 80).
The heart—the most private place in the novel—becomes the central
text, rather than words, which are increasingly inadequate for expressing Evelina's true, private feelings.

Evelina's strategy against Villars resembles the one she uses against society itself. Just as she tries to obscure her private life by preserving her anonymity and maintaining silence, so here she resists "exposure" by obscuring with silence her emotional life, spending considerable time in "my own room" and struggling, as Villars puts it, "to hide what it should seek to participate." It is interesting that he, like society at large, is only comfortable with her "participation"—and he resists, with the same intrusive curiosity, Evelina's intention to conceal herself.

Although Evelina declares in Letter 60 that "Concealment . . . is the foe of tranquillity," it is not the last time he will use this weapon. One of her most effective uses of it is against Orville—even after they are engaged. The power she enjoys and the privacy that concealment allows her is preferable to the exposure to Orville of both her lineage problem and the Macartney situation. Evelina notes her sense of "treachery, of revealing the story, and publishing the misfortunes and poverty of Mr. Macartney; who has an undoubted right to my secrecy and discretion" (Letter 66). " 'You shall tell me nothing you would wish to conceal, . . .' 'There is *nothing*, my Lord, I wish to conceal,—to *postpone* an explanation is all I desire' " (Letter 76). It is obvious in these lines how Evelina uses language as a sort of smoke screen.

In this context one notices in Evelina's penultimate letter to Villars that Orville is called the "loved owner" of her heart; "You are now," murmurs Orville upon reading the consent, "all my own!" Interestingly, however, Evelina also uses this letter as her last opportunity to assert her own, private identity: "Now then, therefore, for the first—and probably the last time I shall ever own the name, permit me to sign myself, Most dear Sir, your gratefully affectionate, EVELINA BELMONT" (Letter 82).

Yet the reflexiveness of her former pseudonym, Anville, is not left behind with her old, anonymous, life. Her final name, Orville, is itself similar to Anville and Villars. This is all the more notable in light of Evelina's explicit comparisons of these two men, and especially in light of the momentarily unclear identity, in the novel's final line, of the "best of men" into whose arms she would be conducted. The near-interchangeability of names clearly has something to do with the apparent interchangeability of father figures in this novel.

Fanny Burney's original inscription, dedication, and preface were all published, of course, like the novel, anonymously. Professional anonymity was a way of protecting one's reputation—and one's privacy. And one needn't look far to discover in Burney's own jour-

nals an almost obsessive fear of being identified as the author of
Evelina:

> [This intelligence gave me the utmost uneasiness,—I fore-
> saw a thousand dangers of a discovery;—I dreaded the indis-
> creet warmth of all my confidents,] . . . [In truth I was quite
> sick with apprehension.]

Burney evidently saw her novel as an "exposure" of herself to the
public:

> I have an exceeding odd sensation, when I consider that it is
> now in the power of *any* and *every* body to read what I so
> carefully hoarded even from my best friends, till this last
> month or two,—and that a work which was so lately lodged,
> in all privacy of my bureau, may now be seen by every
> butcher and baker, cobbler and tinker, throughout the three
> kingdoms.

At the same time, of course, she silently thrilled at hearing or reading
favorable reviews:

> I must own I suffered great difficulty in refraining from
> laughing upon several occasions,—and several times, when
> they praised what they read, I was upon the point of saying—
> "You are very good!" and so forth, and I could scarce keep
> myself from making acknowledgements, and bowing my
> head involuntarily.

Burney's obsession with privacy and concealment are evident as early
as her juvenile journal "Addressed to a Certain Nobody," which opens
with a self-exhortation: "A Journal in which I must confess my every
thought, must open my whole heart!" Here, as in the novel, a journal,
a text, is seen as the ultimate "private space"—a room for one's heart-
felt emotions and most private thoughts. The text itself becomes, like
Miss Mirvan, a second self. As an appropriate addressee, therefore,
Burney finds only herself—or rather, the anonymous "Nobody":

> Since to Nobody I can be wholly unreserved—to Nobody
> can I reveal every thought, every wish of my heart, with the
> most unlimited sincerity . . . For what chance, what acci-
> dent can end my connections with Nobody. No secret *can* I
> conceal from Nobody, and to Nobody can I be ever
> unreserved.

Burney seems to have lived in constant fear that her journal and her novel-in-progress would be discovered. And the journal was discovered finally, by her father, who, adding to her mortification, said nothing of it until she had stood silently at his study doorway for at least a half-hour. "All I can say for myself," Burney adds in her diary, "is that I have always feared discovery, always sought concealment, and always known that no success should counterbalance the publishing of my name."

Far from "owning" or acknowledging *her* authorial identity, Burney does everything possible to obscure that identity: "Without name, without recommendation, and unknown alike to success and disgrace, to whom can I so properly apply for patronage, as to those who publicly profess themselves inspectors of all literary performances?" Like Evelina herself, Burney seeks admission into a society to which she *must* expose herself, but she is capable of doing so only while "happily wrapped up in a mantle of impenetrable obscurity."

It is consistent with the novel as a whole that Fanny Burney ultimately defers entirely to male judgment; the very act of authorship is displaced upon Dr. Burney: "Oh, Author of my being!—far more dear / To me than light." The first three stanzas of the inscription suggest that perhaps the only truly acceptable literary effort would be one that simply traced "thy num'rous virtues"; she becomes then not Author, but mere "Recorder of thy worth." It is not only fear of Dr. Burney's disapproval that is registered in *Evelina*'s introductory material; it is also the fear of disapproval from her father's literary counterparts—the critics. Burney acknowledges the right of both her father and the critics not only to censure but also to censor, or silence, her work. "Concealment is the only boon" she claims in the original inscription; obscurity, for Burney as for her Evelina, is always the best defense.

Evelina's Deceptions:
The Letter and the Spirit

Julia L. Epstein

Fanny Burney had a compulsion to write—she repeatedly refers to a writing "mania" in her journals and letters. At the same time, she understood that for her time and circumstances, to write was to defy convention, and this understanding emerges in covert and coded ways in her fiction. In particular, the epistolary *Evelina or the History of a Young Lady's Entrance into the World* (1778) can be interpreted as a treatise on the appropriate uses of language for young women in the late eighteenth century, and on the methods by which that apparent appropriateness may be manipulated to subvert social oppression. This first novel maps the terrain of eighteenth-century social decorum, in relations between the sexes and between youth and age, as a minefield waiting to explode. Like Burney's third novel, *Camilla; or, A Picture of Youth* (1796), *Evelina* contains tongue-tied and sabotaged conversations, misread gestures, and unfinished communications. Evelina's letters represent an expressly "feminine" art: the art of coaxing, flattering, and mystifying; the art of requesting and granting permission or forgiveness; and the verbal ingenuity of the woman whose survival depends upon her appearing to remain ingenuous and innocent, and whose only tool of power lies in her use of language to manipulate both her situation and the way it is presented to others. In *Evelina*, Burney excavates beneath the eighteenth-century social virtues of "feminine" decorum and artlessness professed by her heroine to a gritty and subterranean exposure of the language that controls both propriety and rebellion against it.

At the age of sixty, the Marquise de Lambert inaugurated one of the most important literary salons in Paris, and speculated on the power available to women in the eighteenth century:

> They tell us in the cradle: You are not capable of anything, don't concern yourself with anything, you are good for nothing but to be prudent; they told it to our mothers, who believed it and repeated it to us. . . . What other resource did they leave us but the miserable function of pleasing? Our coquetry comprises all our wealth.

Fanny Burney's first heroine uses that same metaphor of "wealth" to describe her progress from relative poverty and an uncomfortably ambiguous social identity to the acquisition of an acceptable identity and status in the social world. "Dearly, indeed," she tells her guardian, "do I purchase experience!" Yet despite her claim to worldly experience, until recently critics have tended to view Evelina as a complacent and naive victim of circumstances conveniently contrived by her creator. Evelina has been called, for example, a "priggish mouse," a "nervous filly," and a "flustered goose." It is precisely her circumstances, however, that require her to be neither pathetic nor docile, in fact require her to be none of these domesticated or barnyard creatures. Burney's *Evelina* is more than merely a comedy of manners and errors. It should be read, instead, as a feminist novel of education, and as the story of a young woman whose nefariously ambiguous position forces her to learn how to keep others from making decisions for her. It is a story, then, of private sovereignty and self-determination.

The major clue to how Evelina understands and responds to her situation lies in the epistolary documents with which the novel presents us. Letter-writing in *Evelina* is a synecdochic gesture: it stands, in miniature, for the tenuous and danger-fraught communication process between authority and its charge, between the empowered and the powerless. A well-behaved young woman, Evelina knows, must be innocent and artless, and the "art" of letter-writing—that "feminine" accomplishment for cultured ladies—should reflect this. But innocence and artlessness get Evelina continually into trouble, so self-preservation demands that she replace those traits with experience as fast as she can. Her guardian, the Reverend Arthur Villars, affects not to understand this exigency (though Evelina's grandmother Madame Duval knows and promotes it); so as Fanny Burney herself had not wanted to appear studious in public, Evelina also must disguise her burgeoning intelli-

gence about the ways of the fashionable world. Letters are the vehicles
for this deceit and for the rhetorical repossession it engenders. Letters
became an especially licensed mode of writing for eighteenth-century
women writers and their heroines precisely because letter-writing was
a sanctioned female activity. Because it was licensed, the letter also
presented a potential arena for subversion. As a feminine narrative
form, letters pretend to spontaneity and absolute sincerity. But they
can never be utterly sincere, as no crafted piece of writing can be
without artifice. Evelina makes sophisticated use of this potential, as
did Burney herself.

Evelina's rhetorical problems begin with her name, which has
been given her by Villars. It is a version of her dead mother's maiden
name, Evelyn, and Villars also gives her the anagrammatic made-up
surname of "Anville." From birth, then, Evelina's names are absurdist
constructions, neither fully given nor fully family names. Names in a
Burney novel both bestow and withhold identity; they are absolute
signs for the slipperiness of female selfhood and the conflicted play of
female dependence and autonomy in a culture that infantilized its
women. Indeed, the resolution of *Evelina* can only come about when
the complex kinship and authority systems of family and education are
sorted out, and the heroine legally becomes Evelina Belmont Orville,
shedding "Anville" altogether, as she achieves at last a legitimate and
publicly sanctioned name. Evelina turns out, of course, *not* to be the
poor orphan girl: she is the daughter of a wealthy aristocrat, Sir John
Belmont, who had married and then abandoned her mother. But even
after Belmont belatedly recognizes Evelina, no sooner can she claim
the Belmont name, fortune, and social status, than she trades in all
three for the parallel sanctions of marriage to Lord Orville (who has,
significantly, no given name). In fact, although the entire plot seems to
involve intricate ploys to earn back her rightful name and birth identity, only one of the novel's letters is signed "Evelina Belmont"
precisely because Evelina's quest to regain her family and legitimate
"name" is paralleled by a quest to replace those original blood ties, the
instant they are legalized, with ties of her own choice and determination.

Throughout, it is Evelina's connections to key men that matter
most, because only in accordance with those connections can her social
status be ratified. She replaces these men one by one, and quite system-
atically: first her biological father replaces the surrogate affective parent
Villars; then her husband takes over for both father figures. Indeed,
Evelina seeks Villars's initial approval of Lord Orville by comparing

the two men. "I sometimes imagine, that, when his youth is flown, his vivacity abated, and his life is devoted to retirement, he will, perhaps, resemble him whom I most love and honour," she writes of the hero to her guardian, so the lineage (and the circularity) of mentors is clear ("Orville," after all, is another version of "Anville"—and/or an equivalence). The anxiety Evelina expresses throughout the narrative about how to "sign" her letters—and letters depend upon their signatures for authority and credibility, a fact dramatized by her libertine persecutor, Sir Clement Willoughby, with his forgery at the end of volume 2—provides, then, the impetus she requires to undertake and to complete her search.

Evelina's "signature," the authority by which she signs the correspondence that constitutes her narrative, also prefigures the problematic naming of Burney's other heroines, especially Cecilia Beverley, whose protofeminist need not only to keep her own name upon marriage but also to impose it on her husband so embroils her romance with Mortimer Delvile, and Juliet Granville of *The Wanderer*, whose disguised name (L. S./Ellis) is as "made up" as in Evelina's initial appellation. When Evelina sheds her superfluous false surname Anville—that scrambled repetition of Evelina—to take on a public name, it doesn't matter whether she goes by the legitimating "Belmont" whose respectability the novel's plot wins her. She only needs that momentarily in order to sanction her marriage, and yet another name change. Belmont and Orville, fashionable names both, are interchangeable. The name, indeed, serves metonymically as social propriety; Madame Duval, for example, "told them, that she had it in her head to *make something* of me, and that they should soon call me by another name than that of Anville, and yet that he was not going to have the child married, neither." The fashionable Mrs. Beaumont embarrasses Evelina with a barrage of questions about which of the Anvilles—those in the North or those in Lincolnshire—she is related to. And her worst mortification, when her vulgar cousins the Branghtons finagle the use of Lord Orville's carriage in a rainstorm, comes most acutely from the misuse of her *name*, which she had urged them not to speak aloud. She upbraids Tom with particular zest when he gains access to Orville by mentioning "Miss Anville." " 'Good God,' " she expostulates in fury, " 'and by what authority did you take such a liberty?' "

Evelina's mother had had her own obessions with names and titles, though she did not hesitate to sign her posthumously delivered letter to her profligate husband "Caroline Belmont": "Shall I call you by the loved, the respected title of husband?" she asks him. "No, you disclaim it!—the father of my infant?—No, you doom it to infamy! —the lover who rescued me from a forced marriage?—No, you have yourself betrayed me!—the friend from whom I hoped succour and protection?—No, you have consigned me to misery and destruction!" Caroline negatively defines each of the titles she rejects for Belmont. And when her father beholds Evelina for the first time, he identifies her with the exclamatory " 'My God! does Caroline Evelyn still live!' " Both Evelina and Polly Green, the impostor daughter Belmont has raised as his own child, are married within a week of Belmont's recognition, prompting Mrs. Selwyn, Evelina's chaperone at Bristol, to remark, " 'if either of you have any inclination to pull caps for the title of Miss Belmont, you must do it with all speed, as next week will take from both of you all pretensions to it.' " Lord Orville introduces Evelina as Miss Belmont to his sister Lady Louisa, then immediately announces " 'whom I hope shortly . . . to have the happiness of presenting to you by yet another name.' " Captain Mirvan greets her with " 'So, Miss Belmont, I wish you joy; so I hear you've quarrelled with your new name already?' " In the midst of all this name-changing, Evelina writes a curt letter to Willoughby, and "Not knowing by what name to sign, I was obliged to send it without any." To this point, Evelina's letters have gone partially unsigned, as "Evelina———," on the grounds, she writes Villars in her initial letter to him, that "I cannot to *you* sign *Anville*, and what other name may I claim?" Only one letter to Villars is signed "Evelina Belmont," and with this closing, "Now then, therefore, for the first—and probably the last time I shall ever own the name, permit me to sign myself": a strange fate (ownership as both admission and possession) for the name whose acquisition has been the novel's driving force.

The crucial issue in *Evelina*'s use of letters and signatures is reader- and writer-context. The recognized conventions of eighteenth-century epistolary fiction and the general tone of comedic benevolence cultivated by Fanny Burney in *Evelina* make it too easy to forget that Villars, the primary reader of Evelina's letters as well as her guardian, has decision-making along with moral power over her. He represents the source of all permission. If she angers or offends him, all is lost—on his approval rests her tenuous foothold in polite society. We cannot expect, then, that her letters to this guardian, to whom she writes most regularly and frequently, will be straightforward. She has no choice but to edit them carefully. Most critics of *Evelina* have ignored this crucial facet of Evelina's narrative strategy. She is a storyteller with an ulterior motive. The covert distortions her self-editing necessarily prompts control the narrative Evelina's letters ultimately produce.

The epistolary format of the novel, an expected enough fictional mode in 1778, allows Burney to play with tone, sincerity, and narrative truth. Evelina uses her letters as emissaries to her guardian: they plead her case without offending her judge. Each volume of *Evelina* presents a problem of education—both in how to behave and in how to phrase and organize an account of one's behavior—and this education ultimately serves to train Evelina in the procedures for conducting a search for a father, a husband, a name, and a proper and publicly sanctionable social status. In volume 1, she learns aristocratic manners: how to refuse to dance at an assembly without creating gossip; what to wear and where to sit at the opera; how to distinguish the fashionable from the vulgar. In volume 2, she joins the London middle class, learns the dangers of the city and its pleasure gardens for an unescorted woman, and applies her new knowledge of social rules, now sometimes to her own advantage. By volume 3, she actually controls the behavior of others towards her and determines her own social position. From the outset, however, she has a facility with words and their arrangement, though her education also makes her more adept with language's tyrannies and its argumentative potential.

In Villars's initial account of Evelina to Lady Howard, he describes her as "this artless young creature, with too much beauty to escape notice, . . . too much sensibility to be indifferent to it; but . . . too little wealth to be sought with propriety by men of the fashionable world." Villars seems most concerned with the "female difficulties" articulated by Burney's last heroine, Juliet Granville of *The Wanderer*, who represents a radically politicized and economically extreme evolution of Evelina's character. Juliet concludes of the woman alone: "Her honour is always in danger of being assailed, her delicacy of being offended, her strength of being exhausted, and her virtue of being calumniated." These statements quite succinctly express the bind Burney's heroines find themselves in. But Villars focuses on a side issue: while not wealthy before Belmont accepts her, she is never poverty-stricken, and with the addition of Madame Duval's considerable worth to the legacy Villars intends for her, financial exigency does not dog her—by Branghton or the dull Mr. Smith (Samuel Johnson's favorite character in the novel), for example, she is seen as a plum catch for a wife. What does make Evelina an unacceptable match for a man of fashion is her ambiguous family connection and lack of a legal name, a problem Villars consistently evades. Evelina must maintain her sensibility and apparent artlessness, and slip around the social problems her pseudo illegitimacy poses. She must, therefore, distort her accounts to Villars.

Evelina's relation to her guardian of her adventures in the "world" remains deliberately incomplete. Sometimes she uses Richardson's "writing-to-the-moment" stance, writing with one arm while the other is up to its elbow in social crises ("I can write no more now. I have hardly time to breathe") to achieve this; letters get lost, crossed, or abandoned ("I could not forbear writing a few words instantly on my arrival; though I suppose my letter of thanks for your consent is still on the road"); she apologizes for her lack of "style" and rhetorical polish ("pray excuse the wretched stuff I write, perhaps I may improve by being in this town, and then my letters will be less unworthy your reading"); long intervals are left blank and unaccounted for ("The first fortnight that I passed here, was so quiet, so serene, that it gave me reason to expect a settled calm during my stay; but if I may now judge of the time to come by the present state of my mind, the calm will be succeeded by a storm, of which I dread the violence"); and, finally, in the ultimate disclaimer of overwrought emotion and rhetorical intensity, she writes of the plot's climactic romantic confrontation: "I cannot write the scene that followed, though every word is engraven on my heart"—for the first time taking the female prerogative of private sentimental discretion to announce to Villars just what it is she is concealing. Letter-writing itself becomes one of Evelina's chief activities: "I have a vast deal to say, and shall give all this morning to my pen. As to my plan of writing every evening the adventures of the day, I find it impracticable; for the diversions here are so very late, that if I begin my letters after them, I could not go to bed at all." Although Evelina claims to be sending her guardian a minutely detailed journal, a comprehensive account of her "entrance into the world," in fact, she maintains the selective privilege of the creative artist throughout her narrative. She writes from the angle from which she chooses Villars to view her adventures; she adopts a discourse of innocence arrested and then tutored; and he reads ultimately only what she wants him to know.

One sign of the careful editing process Evelina uses in her letters to Villars is the difference in tone and style between these letters, which make up the bulk of the narrative, and the several others she has occasion to write during the course of the novel. The most important of these other letters are addressed to her friend, confidante, and alter ego Maria Mirvan, who Evelina calls "my second self" and "the friend of my heart." They contain hints about Evelina's analysis of the journal she has been deliberately and self-consciously composing for Villars. The letters to Maria mark tonal shifts in the narrative, and serve as meditational breaks from the newsy, fast-paced yet discursively bloodless letters Evelina sends to her guardian. She never tells him, for example, that London is "where I lately enjoyed so much happiness," a "gay and busy" place. She divulges her real thoughts and feelings only to Maria, even telling Villars "I conceal nothing from her, she is so gentle and sweet-tempered, that it gives me great pleasure to place an entire confidence in her."

Evelina writes to Maria mostly from Berry Hill, Villars's country home (there is one transcribed letter from London, along with one from Bristol Hotwells—more from Bristol are alluded to but not included in the novel). Evelina is, quite simply, bored and restless at Berry Hill in Villars's company. She needs a female friend, and Villars, she admits, filial tenderness notwithstanding, will no longer do. "Perhaps," she writes to Maria, "had I first seen *you*, in your kind and sympathizing bosom I might have ventured to have reposed the secret of my soul." Villars, clearly, does not have all of Evelina's confidence, and it is not surprising that a seventeen-year-old girl should withhold some of her feelings from the apparently kindly but dangerously ineffectual and naively judgmental elderly country parson who has raised her. This lack of complete trust in Evelina's account to Villars, understandable or not, must temper our critical reading of the novel. Most critics have, like Villars himself, been duped by Burney into believing that Evelina has presented us with the whole historical truth, when the narrative discourse of the novel offers clear evidence to the contrary.

The letters to Maria, unlike those to Villars, are direct, their style colloquial and forthright, their tone unstudied. Explaining her mood to Maria in one of the Berry Hill letters, Evelina writes: "I blush for what I have written . . . but I restrain [my gravity] so much and so painfully in the presence of Mr. Villars, that I know not how to deny myself the consolation of indulging it to you." And to Villars, before recounting yet another social *faux pas*, Evelina explains with feigned contrition: "Will you forgive me, if I own that I have *first* written an account of this transaction to Miss Mirvan?" The forged letter from the underhanded cad Willoughby, on which one of the plot's love complications turns, is indeed communicated to Maria and concealed from Villars. To Maria, Evelina admits that she questions and doubts her own feelings, those same feelings whose purportedly absolute definition constitutes her journal to Villars. To Maria, she explains her masquerade at Berry Hill: "All my thoughts were directed to considering how I might dispel the doubts which I apprehended Mr. Villars had formed, without acknowledging a circumstance which I had suffered so much pain merely to conceal."

At the end of her story in Berry Hill, however, Evelina repents of having concealed her disillusionment about Lord Orville's letter, and vows "an unremitting confidence" to Maria *and* to Villars in future, a vow that validates the novel's third volume. On arrival in Bristol, she tells Maria, "I will continue to write to you, my dear Miss Mirvan, with as much constancy as if I had no other correspondent; tho' during my absence from Berry Hill my letters may, perhaps, be shortened on account of the minuteness of the journal which I must write to my beloved Mr. Villars." The compelled "must" still urges us to weigh Evelina's discourse to her guardian, especially as the final volume witnesses his double displacement by Belmont and Orville. But in fact we do not read another letter to Maria from this point on. The novel refers to replies from Maria which inspire Evelina to unburden herself, but these too, no more than embedded dialogue from her friend, are never transcribed. And we read only one of the letters to Maria from London, which Evelina mentions to Villars: "She [Maria] made me promise to send her a letter every post. And I shall write to her with the same freedom, and almost the same confidence, you allow me to make use of to yourself." When the two friends are reunited at Bristol Hotwells in the last sequence, Evelina writes especially elliptically to her guardian, "I say nothing of our conversation, because you may so well suppose both the subjects we chose, and our manner of discussing them," in a calculated silence. So there is a second novel here, over which *Evelina* rests like a palimpsest—the novel that Evelina's letters and conversations with a peer, another young woman, would comprise.

The opening narrative pretext for the journal to Villars, then, already engages a problem of vocal sincerity, as Evelina appears to participate reluctantly, at least at first, in the production of this narrative. In her initial letter to Villars, she writes: "I am half ashamed of myself for beginning this letter," the first of a series in which she asks his sanction for her plans. The Mirvans, she pretends, have put her up to it, and her opening missive has an express and specific purpose—to secure permission from Villars to accompany the Mirvans to London, an apologetic gesture of request that Evelina repeats throughout the novel. "Decide for me," she tells her guardian here, and later, "think for me, . . . my dearest Sir, and suffer my doubting mind, that knows not which way to direct its hopes, to be guided by your wisdom and unerring counsel." Her manipulations in these apologies and in her effort to appear helplessly dependent upon her guardian's judgment, however, are hidden surely only to Villars. When she writes of the London trip, for example, "pray don't suppose that I make any point of going, for I shall hardly sigh to see them depart without me; though I shall probably never meet with such another opportunity," we can hardly be taken in.

This is Evelina's most apparently ingenuous, even childish, letter, and it employs an oblique address to its recipient. "Well but, my dear Sir," writes Evelina, "I am desired to make a request to you. I hope you will not think me an incroacher; Lady Howard insists upon my writing!—yet I hardly know how to go on; a petition implies a want, —and have you left me one? No, indeed." Guilt manipulations are overt here: "What a happy party! Yet I am not *very* eager to accompany them; at least, I shall be very well contented to remain where I am, if you desire that I should." And she ends with "You will not, I am sure, send a refusal, without reasons unanswerable, and therefore I shall cheerfully acquiesce. Yet I hope—I hope you will be able to permit me to go!" Evelina's subsequent letters all bear expressions of affection for Villars, and some also close with elaborate signatures, but none again matches the fawning and cunning cultivation of this first, which she signs off: "Adieu, my most honoured, most reverenced, most beloved father! for by what other name can I call you? I have no happiness or sorrow, no hope or fear, but what your kindness bestows, or your displeasure may cause." She never calls him "father" again, but it can be argued from this rhetorical overkill that the plot for Evelina depends upon her speaking past the Reverend Mr. Villars. She pretends to act, always, with his implied consent.

"By what other name can I call you?" Villars fits ambiguously into Evelina's world: his surrogate role as her dead mother's champion is an awkward one for both of them. What kind of man orders this heroine's world? Villars's character and his motives are perhaps the least examined in the novel, and critics have dismissed him precisely because they have assumed his benignity. We meet him directly only in his letters to Lady Howard, instead seeing him primarily through the prism of Evelina's address to him, through his admittedly and openly censored and censorious responses of instruction to her, added to the handful of business reports he dispatches to Lady Howard. If he reveals himself at all, it is in these last. At first, he seems to oppose any project to secure Evelina her rightful name and inheritance, an odd stance for one who claims to have her best interests at heart. He disapproves of a lawsuit on the rather prim grounds that such an enterprise is "so violent, so public, so totally repugnant to all female delicacy": it is clear to whose delicacy the procedure is repugnant. He doesn't weigh the possibility that poverty, dependency, namelessness, and placelessness might be even more repugnant to a young woman who has been raised breathing the headily mysterious romantic ether of aristocratic pretensions and abandonment. Villars remarks of his scheme for Evelina: "My plan . . . was not merely to educate and to cherish her as my own, but to adopt her the heiress of my small fortune, and to bestow her upon some worthy man, with whom she might spend her days in tranquillity, cheerfulness, and good-humour, untainted by vice, folly, or ambition." But if Evelina calls him initially her "father" for lack of a more suitable title, he fails to provide her with the first gift of an avowed father: legitimacy. Villars claims her as his property to "bestow" without being able to install her in the patriarchal family system such a bestowal presupposes.

Evelina's anagrammatic namelessness denies her even minimal social respectability, the thing Villars claims most to desire for her protection. Lady Howard accuses him, politely, of "so carefully concealing the birth, name, and pretensions of this amiable girl" that he thereby diminishes her chances for a good marriage (or any marriage at all) because of the "mystery in regard to her birth." Villars refuses, in fact, to aid in any design to convince Sir John Belmont to recognize his daughter: "As to myself," Villars writes petulantly, "I must wholly decline *acting*, though I will, with unwearied zeal, devote all my thoughts to giving counsel: but, in truth, I have neither inclination nor spirits adequate to engaging personally with this man." In other words, he is all talk and no action. Yet when Madame Duval threatens to cut Evelina from her will, we get another story from Villars: "To me, I own, this threat seemed of little consequence . . . but the incertitude of [Evelina's] future fate, deters me from following implicitly the dictates of my present judgment. . . . In short, . . . I was obliged . . . to compromise with this ungovernable woman, by consenting that Evelina should pass one month with her."

His charge, unlike her difficult grandmother, can be "governed." To justify his concession of a month in London with the unsavory Madame Duval, Villars sanctimoniously writes, "But, alas, my dear child, we are the slaves of custom, the dupes of prejudice, and dare not stem the torrent of an opposing world, even though our judgments condemn our compliance!" And we read in the version of this explanation sent to Lady Howard that Villars has, in fact, obeyed custom rather than conscience, and been motivated by a concern for wealth over righteous behavior. He tells his ward to do as he says rather than as he does ("you must learn not only to *judge* but to *act* for yourself") and charges her with his famous threat, "Remember, my dear Evelina, nothing is so delicate as the reputation of a woman: it is, at once, the most beautiful and most brittle of all human things." Samuel Crisp made a similar observation to Fanny Burney (and indeed the "Daddy" /"Fannikins" correspondence of Burney's youth reads at moments like that between Villars and Evelina; Villars has been assumed to be modelled on Crisp): "I will never allow you to sacrifice a grain of female delicacy for all the wit of Congreve and Vanbrugh put together," Crisp told Burney of her comedy-writing. Burney herself more knowingly echoed this stance in an oft-quoted remark from a letter to Crisp: "I would a thousand times rather forfeit my character as a writer, than risk censure of ridicule as a female."

"The reputation of a woman" receives its severest setbacks from the behavior and social presentation of Evelina's assertive grandmother. Madame Duval is a woman Villars calls violent, vulgar, ignorant of propriety, and in general "by no means a proper companion or guardian for a young woman." If he is unwilling to deprive Evelina of this dubious woman's fortune, why does he so readily refuse to help her get the much larger one to which she is legally entitled? In fact, Evelina's economic situation is not as lean as the pathetic adjectives attributed to her would make it seem. Though Madame Duval threatens and expostulates, her contrition over abandoning Evelina's mother makes it unlikely that she will really cut off her granddaughter, and her money, bourgeois and inelegant though its owner may be, is not an inconsiderable sum, its provenance Evelina's cowardly but economically correct grandfather. Villars, too, if he sincerely intends Evelina to inherit from him (and he has no other visible heirs), has a respectable country parson's income to bestow. The problem, as Villars understands it, is not how to claim Evelina's rightful material possessions; rather, it turns on how to possess the aristocratic status, blue blood, and titled pretensions and equipages Belmont's name and wealth can confer.

To solve this problem, Villars passes Evelina to the authority of four successive women, a curious gesture in itself from a man who has argued that approaching Belmont would be "repugnant to all female delicacy"—Lady Howard, Mrs. Mirvan, Madame Duval, and Mrs. Selwyn. It is through their delegated power that Evelina eventually makes her plea to her biological father. Lord Orville describes Mrs. Mirvan as "a true feminine character." Madame Duval, in contrast, is a splendid creation of surliness and good-natured ill-breeding. Finally, it is under the guidance of Mrs. Selwyn, whose manners and understanding Evelina dubs "*masculine*," that she wins both her father's recognition and the hand of Lord Orville. Villars passively leaves Evelina to the counsel of women, and women are the agents in all the novel's major events. Even Lady Belmont, long dead, speaks forcefully from the grave on Evelina's behalf through her posthumous letter to her husband. Only Villars, of all her mentors, abandons Evelina entirely to her own devices by refusing to run direct interference for her.

What has Villars taught Evelina to prepare her for adult womanhood and to arm her against the deceptions of the fashionable world, and how does he react to her independent decisions? He rebukes her, from the outset, for her efforts to survive in the London social jungle. Yet the only weapon he arms her with is a knowledge of courtly-genteel language, the sign of her inherited social class. Of her two assembly fiascos, he writes: "I am sure I need not say, how much more I was pleased with the mistakes of your inexperience at the private ball, than with the attempted adoption of more fashionable manners at the ridotto. But your confusion and mortifications were such as to entirely silence all reproofs on my part." That's not reassuring, and when Villars does get around to giving advice rather than reproaching, his pronouncements are not of much practical use. "Alas, my child," he laments, "the artlessness of your nature, and the simplicity of your education, alike unfit you for the thorny paths of the great and busy world." When Belmont appears to disown Evelina in his first letter to Lady Howard, Villars consoles her with exhortations to refrain from claiming her birthright while warning her with just the opposite admonition—to avoid passivity—with regard to Willoughby: "you cannot, my love, be too circumspect; the slightest carelessness on your part, will be taken advantage of. . . . It is not sufficient for you to be reserved; his conduct even calls for your resentment." Nevertheless, having commanded Evelina to inaction toward her father and vehemence against Willoughby, Villars himself capitulates with open cowardice and venality to Madame Duval, by far the most unsettling of Evelina's tormentors because the most legitimate and the most perspicacious about the younger woman's position as a statusless woman; Evelina's plight in some ways resembles that of her grandmother, who is a foreigner travelling with a man to whom she is not married.

So how does Evelina acquire an education in the course of the novel? Some of her most telling because least well guarded reflections come before her schooling has quite begun—and, needless to say, what she learns, to Villars's chagrin, are the rules of fashionable social behavior and coquetry. Burney uses her initial innocence about these rules as an effective cover for recounting social engagements with biting satire. Here, for example, is Evelina at her first ball, describing her outrage at being on display and powerless, an outrage that occasions her first social blunder when she acts instinctively on it without regard for what is "proper":

> The gentlemen, as they passed and repassed, looked as if they thought we were quite at their disposal, and only waiting for the honour of their commands; and they sauntered about, in a careless indolent manner, as if with a view to keep us in suspense. . . . I thought it so provoking, that I determined, in my own mind, that, far from humouring such airs, I would rather not dance at all, than with any one who should seem to think me ready to accept the first partner who would condescend to take me.

Shortly after this scene, the egregious but put-upon fop Lovel minces forward and, not only does Evelina refuse to dance with him, setting up her first major gaffe, but she is also at pains to conceal her laughter. This is more than merely a comment on the social ineptitude of an innocent country girl in the city, and more than mere harmless social satire. Burney, too, is outraged that a woman should not be at liberty to turn down a man, and while she makes her heroine initially ignorant of the complex implications of saying no to a man who is merely unappealing to her, she doesn't make her stupid. Evelina's assessment that she has been displayed as merchandise is accurate, and her resentment justified. And the merchandising of Evelina, though less overtly unfolded, comprises the novel's central subject: both Evelina and her creator recognize that.

How to avoid being condescended to as a formal object—which for a young woman in the eighteenth century amounts to how to say "no"—becomes a pressing issue for Evelina. By her second assembly, a ridotto, she has learned that she will not be able to make her own choices, to get away simply with saying "no" to one man and "yes" to another. So this time she claims to have been previously engaged. When this too gets her into trouble, and turns Willoughby into her persecutor, she recognizes both the ridiculousness and the rigidity of the proper forms she is expected to follow, and of Willoughby's claim to offense: "I turned away from this nonsense," she writes, "with real disgust." She goes on to demonstrate: " 'Indeed, Sir,' said I very seriously, 'I must insist on your leaving me' " and finally, " 'You have tormented me to death; you have forced me from my friends, and intruded yourself upon me, against my will, for a partner,' " though she does not yet know how to prevail against this male assertion of forced control in Willoughby's manipulation of the rules of public manners. Evelina concludes this sequence by telling Villars, "I am too inexperienced and ignorant to conduct myself with propriety in this town, where everything is new to me, and many things are unaccountable and perplexing."

Oddly, neither Evelina nor Villars takes responsibility for this ignorance: she has never had access to simple social customs that concern public relations between the sexes. Villars's passivity on this issue makes him a conspirator, under the guise of protecting her, in the blindfolding of Evelina. She needs to learn for herself, which she does. In volume 2, faced with Madame Duval's insistence that she go to the Hampstead assembly with the importunate and self-absorbed Mr. Smith, she puts her hard-won knowledge to use and avoids having to dance with this would-be beau: "Mr. Smith teazed me till I was weary of resistance; and I should at last have been obliged to submit, had I not fortunately recollected the affair of Mr. Lovel, and told my persecutor, that it was impossible I should dance with him, even if I wished it, as I had refused several persons in his absence." Mr. Smith serves as a kind of inspiration to Evelina. She tells Villars that "the extreme vanity of this man makes me exert a spirit which I did not, till now, know that I possessed: but I cannot endure that he should think me at his disposal": the same word she had used at her first ball—"disposal." Willoughby, too, who compromises Evelina in his carriage in volume 1, comes in for his rebuke from her in volume 3. When he tries to use fashionable rhetoric to manipulate her, she replies, " 'Sir Clement,' cried I, angrily, 'you have no right to make any conditions.' " It is possible, finally, to say "no" and get away with it. But, as Evelina herself has put it, "dearly, indeed, do I purchase experience!" and her purchases are made, ultimately, in the marketplace of the eighteenth-century's gender economy.

This economy dictates that when Evelina needs a man's advice—when the counsel of Mrs. Mirvan or Mrs. Selwyn is unavailable or incomplete—she must cajole, flatter, and manipulate, all with apparent innocence and real charm, to get it. In a cunning appeal to Lord Orville, she announces:

> "There is no young creature, my Lord, who so greatly wants, or so earnestly wishes for, the advice and assistance of her friends, as I do; I am new to the world, and unused to acting for myself,—my intentions are never wilfully blameable, yet I err perpetually!—I have, hitherto, been blest with the most affectionate of friends, and, indeed, the ablest of men, to guide and instruct me upon every occasion;—but he is too distant, now, to be applied to at the moment I want his aid;—and *here*,—there is not a human being whose counsel I can ask!"

We have to remember a number of things as we read this double-edged speech. Evelina transcribes it in a letter to Villars, and her impressive achievement here is that she manages to flatter Villars and Lord Orville simultaneously while all along cultivating the appearance of artless ingenuousness and charming pathos in her own self-presentation. Evelina is, among other things, quite a mistress of rhetorical seduction. It seems clear that she requires all the verbal art of which she is capable to tell the tale of her adventures in search of a father and husband to a man who wishes to play both roles for her without formally taking on either one and who has deliberately, therefore, absented himself from participating in her welfare, yet to whom she feels indebted. The duplicity this situation breeds must be continually taken into account in reading Evelina's letters.

Susan Staves has analyzed the dangerous world Evelina's situation places her in, and perceptively writes that Evelina "begins as a delicate young girl and seems to think her problem is principally that she will be thought to be indelicate, rather than that she will actually become so." That expresses the crux of eighteenth-century morality and sensibility, especially for women: it doesn't matter what Evelina actually must become to get past the difficulties her denied birth and wealth present her with. She seeks social respectability, and what matters for that is what people think. What people think and gossip about, we all know, frequently depends upon the success of disguises and subterfuge and does not bear any necessary relation to the truth. So one observation we can make is that the accepted critical interpretation of "poor, dear, innocent Evelina" both within and outside the margins of this text—the image of the diminutive, flustered, silly and naive domestic pet—represents Evelina's success in controlling public opinion and maintaining the outward forms of modesty and artlessness against all odds. Her brief encounter with the Marylebone women of pleasure underscores this principle of appearance: what frightens her about these women is that they are so transparently *what they are*, that they offer no attempt at disguise. Mary Wollstonecraft put it well: "It is vain to expect virtue from women till they are, in some degree, independent of men; . . . Whilst they are absolutely dependent on their husbands they will be cunning, mean, and selfish." And Patricia Meyer Spacks has pointed out that "Female innocence . . . is male oppression"—the innocent woman makes social blunders because she is forced to act out her innocence in a world where the crucial element for social survival, particularly for women, derives from Lord Chesterfield's notion of "decorum."

Burney places her heroines repeatedly in predicaments that require them either to unmask themselves and risk social censure or to be disastrously misunderstood, yet their challenges to the social order can never be fully open or direct. In the dedicatory epistle that prefaces *The Wanderer*, Burney provides some clues about her analysis of the distortions in narrative voice that Evelina, of necessity, must embed in her letters. The novel, she asserts,

> is, or it ought to be, a picture of supposed, but natural and probable human existence. It holds, therefore, in its hand our best affections; it exercises our imaginations; it points out the path of honour; and gives to juvenile credulity knowledge of the world, without ruin, or repentance; and the lessons of experience, without its tears.

Evelina purchased her experience dearly; Burney wants to provide it to others at the simple price of a printed book. Walter Allen [in *The*

English Novel], disparagingly and quite unfairly, calls this social element in Burney's theory of the novel a "femininization," a term that he uses to mean "a diminution of range" in relation to what he terms the "masculine" and "expansive" works of novelists such as Henry Fielding and Tobias Smollett. The only world open to Burney's heroines, Allen says, is the world that is "accessible to a conventionally brought up upper-middle-class young lady constantly chaperoned." Samuel Johnson had made the same observation, but in the form of a compliment. "No writer so young and inexperienced," he wrote, "had ever seen so deeply into character, or copied the manners of the time with more accuracy." And Burney herself answered that charge in a 1778 diary entry:

> Perhaps this [writing *Evelina*] may seem a rather bold attempt . . . for a female whose knowledge of the world is very confined, and whose inclinations, as well as situation, incline her to a private and domestic life. All I can urge is, that I have only presumed to trace the accidents to which a "young woman" is liable. I have not pretended to show the world what it actually *is*, but what it *appears* to a girl of seventeen:— and so far as that, surely any girl who is *past* seventeen may safely do?

Such a "restricted" world, in any case, imposed as it was on large segments of the reading populace, was of interest in itself. But the accusations of narrowness and limitation, accusations that have crippled Burney criticism as until recently they crippled Jane Austen criticism, also explain why Burney's, and Evelina's, narrative art must be duplicitous, and why expanding the range and locating and inscribing alternative kinds of power are so crucial to a character as circumscribed in options as in Evelina "Anville" Belmont Orville.

Evelina does not, of course, triumph fully over the patriarchial social order that commands her submission and her duplicity. She does not manage to overturn that order; what she achieves is a measure of personal autonomy and control *within* the confines of "acceptable" social behavior for women in the latter part of the eighteenth century. Burney's first heroine is decorous and polite on the surface, but beneath it she is keenly aware of the bondage her decorous behavior implies. Evelina must disguise from Villars her developing attitudes toward the role she is expected to play. As Lady Mary Wortley Montagu complained in 1710 in a letter to Gilbert Burnet, " 'tis look'd upon as in a degree Criminal to improve our Reason, or fancy we have any." It is clear that had Evelina set out openly to communicate a social critique, to "dictate and prescribe," as the novel itself ultimately does, the Reverend Villars and Lord Orville both would have thought her mad. Nevertheless, we watch Evelina successively manipulate the emotions of all the men in the novel, from Villars, Sir John Belmont, and Lord Orville, who make her "thrice-happy" (and give her three names), to Sir Clement Willoughby and Lovel, Mr. Smith, her melodramatic half-brother Macartney, and her grandmother's friend Monsieur DuBois. We can recapitulate the progress Evelina makes in assertive independence: at her first ball, she is incensed that the men "thought we were quite at their disposal," and she is humiliated by that "disposal"; at a later ball, she says of an unwanted suitor that he inspires her to "exert a spirit which I did not, till now, know that I possessed . . . I cannot endure that he should think me at his disposal"; she writes of the seduction ploys of another leering pursuer, "I turned away from this nonsense with real disgust"; and finally, she tells off her worst persecutor in no uncertain terms: " 'Sir Clement,' cried I, angrily, 'you have no right to make any conditions.' " These are the words of a woman who speaks not meekly but in anger, not innocently but with sophisticated and knowing rebellion, not ingenuously but with calculated sharp-tongued cunning.

Chronology

1752   Frances ("Fanny") Burney born in King's Lynn on June 13, daughter of Dr. Charles Burney, organist, musical historian, composer, with friends in literary and aristocratic circles.

1760   Burney family moves to London.

1762   Burney's mother dies.

1767   Burney burns her first novel, *The History of Caroline Evelyn*.

1768   Burney begins her diary "To Nobody" on March 27.

1770   The practice of writing lengthy journal letters to family friend Mr. Crisp and to her sister Susan begins.

1778   *Evelina* is published anonymously and greeted with enthusiastic reviews. Burney's father introduces Fanny to the Thrales.

1778–83   Burney visits Streatham several times, residing for substantial lengths of time with Samuel Johnson and the Thrales.

1779   *The Witlings*, an unpublished comedy, is completed.

1782   *Cecilia* published.

1785   Friendship with Mrs. Delaney begins.

1786   Burney begins court appointment as Second Keeper of the Robes to Queen Charlotte. She resigns in 1791.

1790   Three out of Burney's four tragedies—*Edwy and Elgiva, Hubert De Vere, The Siege of Pevensey*—are completed; the last, *Elberta*, is begun.

1793   Burney marries Alexandre d'Arblay, an exiled French general, in Mickleham on July 28. She also writes *Brief Reflections Relative to the Emigrant French Clergy*.

1794   The d'Arblays' son, Alexander, is born.

1796	*Camilla* published.
1798	An unpublished comedy, *Love and Fashion,* is completed; though accepted for production at Covent Garden, it is never performed.
1801–2	*A Busy Day* and *The Woman-Hater,* two unpublished comedies, are completed.
1802	The d'Arblays live in France during the war with England; they do not return until 1812.
1811	Burney is operated on for cancer.
1814	*The Wanderer* published. Burney's father dies. The d'Arblays move to France again.
1815	Burney flees to Brussels before the advancing Napoleon; d'Arblay joins opposition troops. The d'Arblays are reunited and return to England.
1818	Burney's husband dies.
1823	Burney writes *Narrative of the Illness and Death of General d'Arblay.*
1832	*The Memoirs of Dr. Burney,* the author's father, are published.
1837	Burney's son dies.
1840	Burney dies on January 6 in London; she is buried in Bath near her husband and son.
1843–46	*Diary and Letters of Madame d'Arblay* are published posthumously in seven volumes.
1889	*The Early Diary of Frances Burney* is published in two volumes.

Contributors

HAROLD BLOOM, Sterling Professor of the Humanities at Yale University, is the author of *The Anxiety of Influence, Poetry and Repression,* and many other volumes of literary criticism. His forthcoming study, *Freud: Transference and Authority,* attempts a full-scale reading of all of Freud's major writings. A MacArthur Prize Fellow, he is general editor of five series of literary criticism published by Chelsea House. During 1987–88, he served as Charles Eliot Norton Professor of Poetry at Harvard University.

RONALD PAULSON is Professor of English at The Johns Hopkins University. His books include *Popular and Polite Art in the Age of Hogarth and Fielding, Literary Landscape: Turner and Constable, Book and Play: Shakespeare, Milton, and the Bible,* and *Representations of Revolution.*

SUSAN STAVES teaches at Brandeis. She is the author of *Players' Scepters: Fictions of Authority in the Restoration.*

PATRICIA MEYER SPACKS, Professor of English at Yale University, is the author of *The Adolescent Idea, The Female Imagination,* and *Gossip.*

JUDITH LOWDER NEWTON is Associate Professor of English at La Salle College. She is the author of *Women, Power, and Subversion: Social Strategies in British Fiction* and coeditor of *Sex and Class in Women's History.*

MARY POOVEY, Professor of English at Rutgers University, is the author of *The Proper Lady and the Woman Writer: Ideology as Style in the Works of Mary Wollstonecraft, Mary Shelley, and Jane Austen,* and other studies of eighteenth-century fiction.

JENNIFER A. WAGNER teaches in the Department of English at Yale University.

JULIA L. EPSTEIN is Associate Professor of English at Haverford College. Her essay is part of a forthcoming work on Fanny Burney and the strategies of eighteenth-century women's prose.

Bibliography

Adelstein, Michael E. *Fanny Burney*. New York: Twayne, 1968.

Allen, Walter. *The English Novel*. London: Phoenix House, 1954.

Baker, Ernest A. *The History of the English Novel*. Vol. 5. London: Witherby, 1934.

Bloom, Edward A., and Lillian D. Bloom. "Fanny Burney's Novels: The Retreat from Wonder." *Novel* 12 (1979): 215–35.

Cecil, David. "Fanny Burney's Novels." In *Essays on the Eighteenth Century Presented to David Nichol Smith*, 212–24. 1945. Reprint. New York: Russell & Russell, 1963.

———. *Poets and Story-Tellers*. New York: Macmillan, 1949.

Copeland, Edward W. "Money in the Novels of Fanny Burney." *Studies in the Novel* 8 (1976): 24–37.

Cutting, Rose Maria. "Defiant Women: The Growth of Feminism in Fanny Burney's Novels." *Studies in English Literature* 17 (1977): 519–30.

Dobson, Austin. *Fanny Burney*. New York: Macmillan, 1903.

Edwards, Averyl. *Fanny Burney, 1752–1840; A Biography*. London: Staples Press, 1948.

Gerin, Winifred. *The Young Fanny Burney*. London: T. Nelson, 1961.

Grau, Joseph A. *Fanny Burney: An Annotated Bibliography*. New York: Garland, 1981.

Hemlow, Joyce. "Fanny Burney and the Courtesy Books." *PMLA* 65 (1950): 732–61.

———. *The History of Fanny Burney*. Oxford: Clarendon, 1958.

Hinkley, Laura. *Ladies of Literature*. New York: Hastings House, 1946.

Jeffrey, David M. "Manners, Morals, Magic, and *Evelina*." *Enlightenment Essays* 9 (1978): 35–47.

Kamm, Josephine. *The Story of Fanny Burney*. London: Methuen, 1966.

Kilpatrick, Sarah. *Fanny Burney*. Newton Abbot, U.K.: David & Charles, 1980.

Macaulay, Thomas. "Madame D'Arblay." In *Critical, Historical, and Miscellaneous Essays*. Boston: Houghton, Osgood, 1879.

MacCarthy, Bridget G. *The Female Pen*. New York: William Salloch, 1948.

Malone, Kemp. "*Evelina* Revisited." *Papers on Language and Literature* 1 (1965): 3–19.

Moers, Ellen. *Literary Women*. New York: Pantheon, 1971.

Montague, Edwine, and Louis L. Martz. "Fanny Burney's *Evelina*." In *The Age of*

Johnson: Essays Presented to Chauncey Brewster Tinker, edited by F. W. Hilles. New Haven: Yale University Press, 1949.

Morley, Edith J. *Fanny Burney.* Pamphlet No. 60. The English Association, 1925.

Olshin, Toby. " 'To Whom I Most Belong': The Role of the Family in *Evelina.*" *Eighteenth-Century Life* 6 (1980): 29–42.

Parke, Catharine. "Vision and Revision: A Model for Reading the Eighteenth-Century Novel of Education." *Eighteenth-Century Studies* 16 (1983): 29–42.

Patterson, Emily H. "Family and Pilgrimage Themes in Burney's *Evelina.*" *New Rambler* 18: 41–48.

———. "Unearned Irony in Fanny Burney's *Evelina.*" *Durham University Journal* 36 (1975): 200–204.

Rubenstein, Jill. "The Crisis of Identity in Fanny Burney's *Evelina.*" *New Rambler* 112 (1972): 45–50.

Schrank, Barbara G., and David J. Sapino, eds. *The Famous Fanny Burney.* New York: John Davy. 1976.

Spacks, Patricia Meyer. *The Adolescent Idea: Myths of Youth and the Adult Imagination.* New York: Basic Books, 1981.

———. "The Dangerous Age." *Eighteenth-Century Studies* 11 (1978): 417–38.

———. *Imagining a Self: Autobiography and Novel in Eighteenth-Century England.* Cambridge: Harvard University Press, 1976.

Stowell, Helen Elizabeth. "Fanny Burney." In *Quill Pens and Petticoats: A Portrait of Women and Letters.* London: Wayland, 1970.

Tinker, Chauncey Brewster. *Introduction to Dr. Johnson and Fanny Burney.* London: Andrew Melrose, 1912.

Tompkins, J. M. S. *The Popular Novel in England, 1770–1800.* Lincoln: University of Nebraska Press, 1961.

Voss-Clesly, Patricia. *Tendencies of Character Depiction in the Domestic Novels of Burney, Edgeworth, and Austen: A Consideration of Subjective and Objective Worlds.* Salzburg: Institute für Anglistik und Amerikanistik (University of Salzburg), 1979.

White, Eugene. *Fanny Burney, Novelist: A Study in Technique.* Hamden, Conn.: Shoe String, 1960.

———. "Fanny Burney." In *Minor British Novelists,* edited by Charles Alva Hoyt. Carbondale: Southern Illinois University Press, 1967.

Acknowledgments

Index